ROUTLEDGE LIBRARY EDITIONS: RADIO

Volume 4

WHO'S LISTENING?

WHO'S LISTENING?
The Story of BBC Audience Research

ROBERT SILVEY

Routledge
Taylor & Francis Group
LONDON AND NEW YORK

First published in 1974 by George Allen & Unwin Ltd.

This edition first published in 2017
by Routledge
2 Park Square, Milton Park, Abingdon, Oxon OX14 4RN

and by Routledge
711 Third Avenue, New York, NY 10017

Routledge is an imprint of the Taylor & Francis Group, an informa business

© 1974 George Allen & Unwin Ltd.

All rights reserved. No part of this book may be reprinted or reproduced or utilised in any form or by any electronic, mechanical, or other means, now known or hereafter invented, including photocopying and recording, or in any information storage or retrieval system, without permission in writing from the publishers.

Trademark notice: Product or corporate names may be trademarks or registered trademarks, and are used only for identification and explanation without intent to infringe.

British Library Cataloguing in Publication Data
A catalogue record for this book is available from the British Library

ISBN: 978-1-138-20918-3 (Set)
ISBN: 978-1-315-44344-7 (Set) (ebk)
ISBN: 978-1-138-21250-3 (Volume 4) (hbk)
ISBN: 978-1-138-21568-9 (Volume 4) (pbk)
ISBN: 978-1-315-44424-6 (Volume 4) (ebk)

Publisher's Note
The publisher has gone to great lengths to ensure the quality of this reprint but points out that some imperfections in the original copies may be apparent.

Disclaimer
The publisher has made every effort to trace copyright holders and would welcome correspondence from those they have been unable to trace.

WHO'S LISTENING?

The Story of BBC Audience Research

by Robert Silvey

London   George Allen & Unwin Ltd
Ruskin House   Museum Street

First published in 1974

This book is copyright under the Berne Convention. All rights are reserved. Apart from any fair dealing for the purpose of private study, research, criticism or review, as permitted under the Copyright Act, 1956, no part of this publication may be reproduced, stored in a retrieval system, or transmitted, in any form or by any means, electronic, electrical, chemical, mechanical, optical, photocopying, recording or otherwise, without the prior permission of the copyright owner. Enquiries should be addressed to the publishers.

© George Allen & Unwin Ltd. 1974

ISBN 0 04 384001 9

Printed in Great Britain
in 11 point Baskerville type
by Willmer Brothers Limited
Birkenhead

TO ELSPETH
1905–1968

who did not live to share
the retirement
during which this book was written

Contents

PREFACE		*page* 11
1	Genesis	13
2	The BBC in Labour	28
3	Sampling People	43
4	First Fruits	58
5	Numbering the People	73
6	Audience Research in War-time—I	87
7	Audience Research in War-time—II	103
8	From War to Peace	120
9	P. & D.	134
10	Television: The Last Years of the Monopoly	153
11	Enter ITV	174
12	Post-Pilkington	196
INDEX		217

Preface

Of the making of books, especially by ex-BBC officials, there is no end so how can yet another be justified? I can only plead that my old friend Philip Unwin refused to take 'No' for an answer when he urged me to tell the story of BBC Audience Research. 'After all', he said, 'you started it and were responsible for it for more than thirty years' – which is true – 'it's a story which would interest other people ...' – which he as a publisher was better able to judge than I – '... the way you would tell it' – which was where I really needed persuasion, for though this book begins with Genesis it contains no Revelations. The truth is that the necessary ingredients for revelations never seemed to come my way. Every time a sensational event occurred within the BBC I seemed to be the only man who had not long known that it might happen. Indeed I must sadly conclude that there must have been many highly delectable pieces of gossip which never reached my ears at all.

Some will think it a more serious omission that this book contains so few examples of decisions made as a direct result of audience research findings. To be frank I do not know of many. This is not because the findings of audience research were consistently ignored, my department being nothing but an elaborate façade intended to foster the delusion that the BBC took cognisance of its public. (Had this been so the Corporation, more often hard-up than flush with funds, would long since have called the whole thing off.)

It was rather because audience research findings were rarely, and in the nature of things could seldom be, the only considerations to be taken into account in decision-making. There were always brute facts which could not be wished away; facts like the availability of resources in studios, talent, manpower and money. The probable consequential effects of each decision would have to be weighed; gratifying the wishes of one section of the public might involve depriving another. Due respect had to be paid to the voices of experience and to professional judgements at different levels. But had I not remained convinced that the BBC accepted the view that a public service broadcasting organisation had a duty to take proper account of the opinions and needs of all its many different publics I would not have spent over thirty satisfying years in its service.

This then is simply the story of one specialised BBC activity – part of its housekeeping – seen through the eyes of one who had the good fortune to be closely associated with it for longer than anyone else. It is told chronologically, although not slavishly so, and it includes reflections as well as facts. Although it has at times to come to grips with methodology (a word which my publisher admits only under protest), it is not a textbook of this branch of social research.

My debt to my one-time colleagues is immeasurable. It is the greater for their readiness to allow me to consult documents and for their constant encouragement in the writing of this book. But the responsibility for any errors or omissions is mine alone.

BBC Audience Research has not stood still since I ceased to lead it. There have been developments both in its services and in its methods with which I should have been proud to be associated. Those who wish to know about them will find my successor as ready and as glad to describe them as his predecessor would have been.

R. J. E. S.

1 Genesis

The birthday of BBC Audience Research was 1st October 1936 but, like all birthdays, it had its antecedents. What brought the Corporation to the point of embarking on this activity? And why was I, of all people, chosen to start it?

In the mid-thirties the BBC was going through one of its periodic phases of being in bad odour with much of the popular press, particularly with the then powerful *Daily Mail* whose radio correspondent was Collie Knox. To him, and to others like him, the BBC could do nothing right, in particular they lampooned Reith whose austere Presbyterian personality was to them anathema. Reith, an unquestionably great man to whom British – and indeed world – broadcasting owes an incalculable debt, had the defects of his qualities. That he didn't suffer fools, or those he considered fools, as gladly as a chief executive of a body so exposed to public gaze is wise to do made him God's gift to the Knoxes of the press for nothing makes an attack on an institution more readable than to cast it in personal terms. And they did have a case. The BBC may have been manifestly incorruptible but its policy decisions did seem to be based on its unshakeable conviction that Aunty knew best.

The Corporation had had an officer whose business it was to 'look after' the press but when he departed, under something of a cloud, the Board of Governors decided to elevate Public Relations to the status of a Division – parallel with the existing three Divisions: Programme, Engineering and Administration – and to appoint a man of distinction as its Controller. Hence Sir Stephen Tallents' departure from the GPO to the BBC and his choice, as deputy Controller, of Patrick Ryan from the tough world of commerce.

Moreover, as Asa Briggs has recorded in *The Golden Age of*

*Wireless**, as early as 1930 voices inside the BBC were to be heard expressing their unease at their lack of information about listeners and their reactions to programmes. In that year Val Gielgud, Director of Drama, was writing, '... it must be of considerable disquiet to many people beside myself to think that it is quite possible that a very great deal of our money and time and effort may be expended on broadcasting into a void'. Sporadic social surveys in the field were conducted abroad and were being collated by the BBC's Director of Foreign Relations, Major C. F. Atkinson who, with the backing of another powerful figure in the BBC, Charles Siepmann, pressed for systematic inquiry in Britain. However, such ideas were dismissed as utopian both by some of those who favoured them in principle and by others who openly declared them dangerous. But the climate which had been unpropitious was changing, and when Tallents took up his post he found the subject had been placed firmly on his agenda.

It was no doubt Ryan who suggested that it was surely of relevance to broadcasting that progressive and respectable manufacturers had found market research to be a useful tool. Tallents agreed, though Reith viewed the idea with suspicion. However, Tallents adroitly referred the suggestion to the BBC's General Advisory Council, an impressive body which met quarterly and whose current Chairman was the then Archbishop of York, William Temple, and whose membership had once simultaneously included two Georges – Robey and Bernard Shaw. The G.A.C. blessed the proposal with a cautious resolution stressing its purely experimental tentative character. Tallents and Ryan were authorised to appoint a Listener Research Officer.

While all these deliberations were in progress I was merely one among millions of other anonymous members of the listening public, as totally unknown to virtually all those who were wrestling with these problems as they were, except in name, to me. I had only been a frequent listener for about six years; before that I hadn't had my own 'wireless set', as we then called radio. To be 'with it' at that time you had to be rather

* Asa Briggs, *The History of Broadcasting in the United Kingdom,* Volume 2 (Oxford University Press, 1965).

patronising about broadcasting and certainly supercilious about those who, like the suburban family in Herbert Farjeon's Little Revue, 'Thanked God for the BBC'. (Attitudes linger on; thirty years later Thomas Barman, at his retirement lunch, was to say that he recognised three religions in Britain – Catholics, who ate fish on Fridays; Anglicans, who washed their cars on Sundays, and people who worshipped the BBC and watched *Panorama* on Mondays.)

But though I found BBC-worship a trifle unctuous, I would have been less than honest if I had not acknowledged that I admired the Corporation and owed it a great deal. I was glad radio was run as a public service. That it was a monopoly didn't worry me: I was prepared to judge it on its performance and its performance suited me. It had given me opportunities to hear an abundance of good music. It brought me news, succinct and well-read and, as far as I could judge, without bias. I enjoyed many of its plays and features, as radio documentaries were then called, and those which didn't interest me I could always avoid. It's 'Talks' policy frequently challenged me with new ideas and enabled me to hear the voices of many whom previously I had only met in print. *The Listener*, to which I had subscribed almost since its inception, seemed to me to be a quite outstanding twopenny-worth. I didn't grudge the time the BBC gave to things which didn't interest me – or which I positively disliked.

Even the famous Reithian Sunday policy didn't leave me personally in a state of impotent fury, though it was causing listeners, particularly working-class listeners, to turn to the continental radio stations broadcasting to Britain for a diet of Forbidden Fruit (dance music, no less) seasoned with advertising. I was not an avid listener to religious broadcasts but the Sunday programmes included enough other material to satisfy my tastes and in this I am sure I was not alone; though equally I was not alone in feeling that Reith's Sunday policy would have to be modified if the BBC were to continue to be a public service in fact as well as in name.

It so happened that I had good reason to know the extent to which in the early thirties the British public was turning to Radio Normandy and Radio Luxembourg on Sundays. At the time I was in the statistical department of the London Press Exchange, one of the larger British advertising agents and there it fell to me to write the report on a survey of listening to continental stations. The L.P.E. needed to have this kind of information for its clients were being increasingly pressed by these stations to include radio advertising in their advertising appropriations. Although it gave me no personal pleasure to record it, nor did it in any way affect my own taste for their programmes, the survey showed that the regular audiences of these stations were substantial and increasing.

Another of my assignments at the L.P.E. may well have played a part in my eventual move to the BBC. Inspired by some recent work in America by the still relatively unknown Dr Gallup, the L.P.E., together with Cadbury Brothers and the *News Chronicle*, decided to conduct a Reader Interest Survey of the British press. It involved interviewing between twenty and thirty thousand people about the daily and evening papers they read. Each was confronted with a virgin copy of the previous day's issue of the paper of his choice and then taken through it, column by column, by an interviewer. The reader was required to indicate which headlines had caught his eye and how much of the ensuing news story or article he had read and which illustrations he had noticed. An analogous procedure was followed with each advertisement.

My job was to organise the analysis of the material and to write the report. The top floor of a rather forbidding warehouse in Clerkenwell was rented for my side of the enterprise and a modest army of clerks was hired – unemployed clerks were pathetically easy to find at that time. I needed an assistant and luckily heard, through the grape-vine, of a young economist recently back from research work at the Brookings Institute in Washington D.C. who was 'looking out for something'. His name was Mark Abrams. What followed was a happy two-year working partnership, a life-long friendship and, for Mark, a distinguished career in social research.

The report on the Reader Interest Survey ran to three fat volumes of statistics, charts and written conclusions. It did not surprise or worry either of us that it was never published. Its three sponsors had invested a great deal in its production and were entitled to reap such competitive advantages from it as they could. I only hope they did. But there was nothing secret about what we were doing and from time to time interested visitors would come to see what we were up to and hear about our methods and approach. Among them was R. S. Lambert, then editor of *The Listener* and later to make the headlines as a plaintiff in the Mongoose Case. At the end of our conversation I said, not very seriously, that I thought it would be fascinating to see similar techniques applied to broadcasting. He gave me a sideways look: 'It would indeed', he said, 'but no one would ever be allowed to do it.'

I gave the incident no more thought but did recall it when, a year or so later I had a phone call from A. P. Ryan. I knew Pat Ryan slightly; he had been Publicity Manager at the Gas Light and Coke Company, one of the L.P.E.'s most valued clients, from which he had gone to the BBC to be Tallents' second-in-command. It was, however, sufficiently unlikely that Pat Ryan would invite me to lunch that I immediately smelt a rat. When we met, at the Garrick Club, Ryan asked me if I minded his having brought Tallents with him. It was a pleasant, easy occasion. The talk flowed freely. While I don't remember quite what we talked about, I know that not once did we ever approach the real subject! I found Tallents charming. In appearance he seemed the prototype of the Senior Civil Servant; neat, dapper, stiff white collar, dark suit and rolled umbrella. He had had an eventful war, finishing up with being British Commissioner in the Baltic States with virtually no troops to back him up. After the war he had returned to the Home Civil Service and had come into the public eye as Secretary of the Empire Marketing Board whose use of advertising, and particularly of the new documentary film, to persuade the public to Buy British, had been imaginative and exciting. When the E.M.B. was dissolved he went to the General Post Office as its first Public Relations Officer, taking the film unit with him. Public Relations as a function, was something new in British life and Tallents was its progenitor.

A few days later Ryan called me again. He sounded almost conspiratorial; could I come to see him at Broadcasting House as he had something to discuss which he could not very well mention on the phone? I went. As by then I expected, he told me that the BBC had decided that it must have some listener research and was looking for someone to set it up. Would I be interested? I was, though my feelings were mixed.

I had a wife, and one son and our second child was imminent. With no private income, money did matter and my salary prospects at the L.P.E. were considerably better than those which would face me at the BBC. In those days the BBC did not attempt to match the salaries of private enterprise. Security and a (contributory) pension, neither of which could be dismissed lightly in the thirties, were put forward as compensations.

I was enjoying being in the advertising world even though, like I suspect many others in advertising, I was periodically assailed by doubts about its social usefulness. To be sure the L.P.E.'s clients were highly respectable enterprises like Cadburys, Recketts and the Gas Light and Coke Company and it was known to have turned away potential clients whose wares were dubious. But my doubts remained and were not wholly silenced by the recognition that advertising was an inevitable concomitant of our private enterprise society for my sympathies were Fabian socialist.

The L.P.E. could afford to attract first-class writers, artists, layout men and executives so I had a stimulating bunch of colleagues whom I should be sorry to leave, and I enjoyed the varied work I was doing. I had heard, too, that the BBC was not a happy ship; that Reith was dictatorial and that Admiral Carpendale, his deputy, had never realised that he had left the quarter decks. Would one find the atmosphere stifling? Fortunately I knew two men who could speak from personal experience and whom I knew I could trust: Leslie Baily (of *Scrapbook* fame) and Roger Wilson (later Professor of Education at Bristol University). Their answers dispelled any misgivings on this score.

Although the arguments for staying where I was were strong, those for accepting Ryan's offer proved stronger – as all along I knew deep down they would. It was a challenge. This was not only because no public service broadcasting system had grappled with listener research before so that one would have to devise suitable methods as well as apply them, but even more because, even though Lambert's remarks could not be taken at face value, it was obvious that the BBC's attitude to listener research would not be the same as that of a commercial enterprise. Commercial enterprises might be, and often were in those days, sceptical about the efficacy of market research, but if once convinced that it did reveal to them what was in most of their customers' minds, how they behaved or why they behaved as they did, were in no doubt about the ends to which such information should be put. The customer was king, or more often queen, and the success of the enterprise depended on gratifying her wishes. Commercially financed broadcasting stations had the same kind of basically simple objective. They could only survive if they pleased their customers – the advertisers. But the position of the BBC was different: as a public service system of broadcasting it had an obligation to the whole of its public which could not be met simply by seeking to satisfy the majority.

Had I not already been a convinced believer in public service broadcasting (and I am still unrepentant) there could have been no question of my taking the job on. But my new colleagues would not know this and might even, because of my background in advertising, be suspicious of me. Protestation on my part would not be enough; I would have to earn their confidence by what I did. The challenge was bracing.

Further, the idea of working for a public service appealed to me. I had never wanted to be a civil servant, probably because no one had told me what entering the Civil Service would mean. Although I had never felt that, as a socialist, I was endangering my immortal soul by working in what is now called the private sector, I knew I should be more at home in a non-profit making enterprise.

So I accepted Ryan's invitation to join the BBC in order to start listener research. (Later the activity became known as audience research and I shall use that term from now on. Incidentally it has never ceased to set my teeth on edge to hear the word 'research' pronounced '*re*search'.)

The way in which the offer came would now be looked at askance and quite rightly so. If the BBC had to make a similar appointment today, someone would have to prepare a draft job specification and get it agreed and graded by the establishment people. Then would come the drafting of an advertisement – which would have to be agreed with the Appointments Department. Internal advertising, that is display on the many notice boards throughout the BBC, would be obligatory so that any existing BBC staff could apply. External advertising – in the press – would only take place if it were thought unlikely that the post could be filled from 'within'. After the closing date for applications a short-list would be prepared by the Appointments Department and the selected candidates summoned to attend a Board. Its Chairman would be drawn from the Appointments Department and its other members would be officials directly concerned with the vacant post but of rank senior to it. If no suitable candidate were found, the whole procedure might have to be repeated.

It was often my lot during my BBC career to have to explain to people who asked me to 'put in a word' for an aspiring nephew that were I to do so it would be more likely to hinder than to enhance the candidate's chances. Although I was often exasperated with the slowness of the procedure for filling posts, I doubt if it could have been more scrupulously fair or better calculated to prevent nepotism. But all this was in the future. At the time I knew perfectly well that the fact that the lot had fallen on me was the merest good fortune. This was before the days when market research had attained the status of a recognised profession. Few were practising it and those who did had no specialised academic training, for there was none to be had. In my case I had stumbled into it almost by chance. I had qualified by evening study as an accountant and the knowledge required to pass my Finals statistics paper would now be considered derisory. But the field suited my temperament and I had taken to it with enthusiasm, though I had to learn on the job. All the same I have often reflected since that, had I had to undergo the appointments procedure which was subsequently set up, my chances of getting the job would have been slim to say the least of it and, who knows, the BBC might have done considerably better.

When I accepted Ryan's invitation to take the post he could

say nothing about salary; I would have to negotiate that with B. E. (later Sir Basil) Nicholls, the Controller of Administration. This I heartily disliked doing; I would have much sooner that they had made me an offer. I found Nicholls tough but kindly and the upshot was that I left the L.P.E. at £600 a year and joined the BBC at £680 – with an assurance that if I measured up to what they wanted this would become £700 at the end of a year and I would be 'established', with the right to participate in their contributory pension scheme. It was not exactly princely but I had no feeling of grievance. For a family man of 31 in 1936, when there were over a million unemployed, it seemed fair enough.

On 1st October, 1936 I presented myself for duty. My mentor in the Public Relations Division was Maurice Farquharson who had fairly recently come from the National Council of Social Service and whose career – interrupted by distinguished war service in the Guards – had included being a master at Bedales and a member of the Old Vic Company. Maurice ultimately became Secretary of the BBC and his 'finest hour' was perhaps his masterly management of the presentation of the Corporation's massive evidence to the Beveridge and Pilkington Committees.

I took an immediate liking to Maurice. We talked the same language and saw things in the same way. Our relationship could easily have been a difficult one for, while I was immediately answerable to him, not only did both Tallents and Ryan take a lively interest in what I was up to but he himself was the first to say that he knew nothing of the methods or rationale of social research. But we worked together in complete harmony and have remained close friends ever since.

Maurice told me that as Broadcasting House, which had only been opened four years before, was overflowing there would be no room for me there. Moreover he wisely said that I might find my feet quicker if at first I shared an office with the Head of the Programme Correspondence Section (H.P.C.S.) which was located in a rented block round the corner in Great Portland Street. I was a little disappointed for there was a glamour about working in B.H., but the arrangement, which in fact only lasted a few weeks, was a good one.

H.P.C.S. was Bobby (R. W. P.) Cockburn, a cousin of Claude Cockburn whose weekly roneod sheet *This Week* was compulsive reading in the thirties. My first meeting with Bobby, who is now the Secretary of the group of wise men who hear complaints against the BBC, startled me. His desk was set cornerwise and behind it was an enormous mountain of empty envelopes. He would remove the contents from his already slit mail and nonchalantly flick the envelope over his shoulder. My ordedly mind was slightly shocked but I soon found this procedure made not the slightest difference to the quality of his work. Routine inquiries and stereotyped letters would be assigned to a secretary to send one of a number of stock, but carefully worded, replies. The minority, which could not be dealt with in this way, would either be coped with by Bobby himself or by one of his several assistants. And it didn't take long to see that they were an able lot. To work in P.C.S. was recognised first apprenticeship to a BBC career. Among those there when I arrived was Oliver Whitley who at his retirement was Director of External Broadcasting.

Finding the right answer to a listener's letter would often mean getting into direct touch with a programme producer and finding what had really been broadcast – which was often not what the writer claimed had been. It sometimes meant softening the draft reply suggested by the infuriated producer exasperated by what he thought to be the writer's boneheadedness, obstinacy or sheer malice. The necessary facts were sometimes difficult to pin down. The queries could be esoteric; sometimes answering one letter would take several days. It was BBC policy to respect its correspondents and to take at least as much trouble in answering them as they had taken to write. This policy paid off. A patient and painstaking reply from P.C.S. to a letter bristling with vituperative indignation would often bring an apologetic response in a wholly different tone so demonstrating that the soft answer could turn away wrath.

Sitting in with Bobby quickly acquainted me with BBC folkways – such as the mysterious initials to whom one wrote memos. They referred to the post the recipient held, not to his name. There was C.P. (Controller, Programmes) for example,

D.O.A. (Director of Office Administration), D.V. (Director of Variety), D.F.D. (Director of Features and Drama) and, somewhat oddly, D.R. (Director of Religion) later to be changed to the more apt D.R.B. (Director of Religious Broadcasts).

I learnt the subtle difference between sending a memo to X 'through' Y, which meant that Y had the right to add his comments or might even send it back with a suggestion for its alteration, and addressing a memo to X 'with a copy to Y', which gave Y no opportunity to comment before X got it but did keep him in the picture, or addressing it to 1.X 2.Y, which meant that Y only received it after X had done so and perhaps had added a minute of his own. I learnt about some personal eccentricities: that P was fierce in writing but mild to meet so that it was always better to go to see him rather than write him a memo, or that as Q tended to somnolence after lunch he was best approached in the morning if he was required to apply his mind to the subject but in the afternoon if you didn't want him to look at the problem too closely.

It was quite a wrench to leave the congenial company of P.C.S. when some rooms were provided for me. They were at the top of a Georgian house in Portland Place on the corner with Duchess Street. They 'adjoined' Broadcasting House only in the sense that you could get there without going into the street. To get to B.H. from my room one went down a flight of stairs, passed through three or four adjoining houses which had been taken over by the BBC and along an enclosed bridge which passed behind the next house which was tenanted by an elderly lady whom the Corporation had the right, but had not the heart, to evict. Between my office and the underground canteen in B.H., to which we repaired for morning coffee and afternoon tea each day, were nineteen swing doors erected in compliance with the no doubt very proper fire prevention requirements of the L.C.C.

I was allocated a secretary from the General Office: Susan Press, a recent recruit from Bristol. She remained my secretary until she left the Corporation to get married twelve years later. No one could have been more loyal, conscientious or efficient. I must have been rather a shock to her at first. I doubt if she had ever had close contact with anyone who was not a high Tory, indeed I suspect that the phenomenon of a middle-class socialist was quite incomprehensible to her. But if she disapproved she never showed it. We rarely discussed politics but a few years later I found she had become a regular reader of the *New Statesman*. From the standpoint of today it will seem extraordinary that, although Susan and I worked closely together, were always good friends and met one another's families, I don't think it ever occurred to either of us to address each other by our Christian names.

Soon after I was allocated an 'assistant'. I don't recall being offered any choice but if I had had good grounds for rejecting Avice Trevelyan, which I had not, no doubt I could have asserted them. Avice had no experience of social research but she was interested in the enterprise and rolled her sleeves up readily enough. I was entertained by the rather endearing arrogance which membership of one of the English intellectual aristocracy seemed to bestow. Avice, who was a good sort, displayed a naive and insatiable curiosity about everything including the personal life of her colleagues. It was as though she turned one over with her foot, albeit in a way which was impossible to resent. When the war came Avice disappeared into the Land Army which somehow seemed appropriate.

Tallents had set up a Listener Research Committee which he told me was primarily intended to bring the rest of the Corporation in on the new activity. He had no intention of prolonging its life indefinitely and indeed I do not recall its meetings to have continued very long. Beside himself as Chairman, Ryan and Farquharson, he invited Charles Siepmann (Director of Programme Planning), Val Gielgud (Director of Features and Drama) both because of his known interest in the subject and to bring in the production side, Leslie Hayes, a senior Engineer, and Major Atkinson whose precise function on the Committee I never succeeded in discovering. He had been Director of Foreign Relations and had expressed interest in audience research. I subsequently discovered that he was an internationally accepted authority on the naval engagements in the American Civil War but the relevance of this to what I was doing seemed a trifle remote.

Val Gielgud was already a nationally known figure for his pioneering work in radio drama. A sardonic figure, his sometimes cutting witticisms and his sword-stick were already legendary inside the BBC. At first I found him somewhat intimidating, but he was always kind to me. His own staff, I found, were devoted to him.

Charles Siepmann had already made his name in broadcasting, first as Deputy to, and then as successor of, Hilda Matheson who was responsible for Talks. I shall always be grateful to Charles for bringing John Macmurray to the microphone some years before. Macmurray, who was Professor of Moral Philosophy at Edinburgh, gave two series of talks, *Reality and Freedom* and *The Modern Dilemma* which so spoke to my condition that I can truly say that they made a lasting difference to the way I looked at life and, I hope, behaved in it. From time to time in the years which followed I was to meet people both here and in America on whom his talks had had a similar effect.

I was never quite clear why Charles left Talks to move to Programme Planning. It was no business of mine so I did not pursue the inquiry with any diligence, but I gather there had been a clash of principle between himself and Reith. If that were so it would not be surprising, for Charles was above all a man of high principle to whom giving way before anything less than what he recognised as a convincing argument would have been inconceivable. A handsome man then in his early forties, with greying hair, blue eyes and a ready smile, he was an attractive figure. He was quick to grasp what the audience research could and could not do and was wholly sympathetic towards its coming. I was sad when, in 1940, he accepted an appointment as Professor of Communications at New York University but on the rare occasions that we met thereafter, either in London or New York, we always took up at exactly the point where we had left off.

My unit continued to be known as the Listener Research Section (of the Home Intelligence Department of Tallents' P.R. Division) until the early days of the war when the Public Relations Division was abolished. We found ourselves transferred to the Programme Division and elevated to the status of a Department. This meant that Maurice Farquharson no longer exercised his benign supervision of our activities; instead I worked direct to B. E. (later Sir Basil) Nicholls who had become Controller, Programmes.

After the war and the revival of television with its own Controller, I pointed out that there was something rather anomalous about a department which served both radio and television being located in the radio hierachy and, moreover, that it was in principle undesirable that a department like ours should be under the authority of those it might have to criticise – though it was true that so far this hadn't caused any difficulty. The point was taken and in the next reorganisation we found ourselves in a new creation, The Secretary's Division, which was first placed under the Director of Administration but was soon put directly under the D-G so that we were completely free from any control by the programme side.

To be sure this was only an internal change. If it were undesirable that the research function should be under the authority of those it served, we ought not to have been inside the BBC at all. Indeed after the introduction of competitive television there were those who said that all audience research ought to be conducted by an autonomous body, serving BBC and ITV equally. But since being part of the BBC never in practice cramped our style or ruffled the surface of our delicate professional consciences, independent institutional status offered no real advantages to set against the considerable disadvantages which it would have entailed – much greater administrative costs and an inevitable attenuation of contact with the departments we worked for.

In one happy sense our transfer to the Secretary's Division was back to Square One for Maurice Farquharson had been appointed The Secretary. When he retired he was succeeded by Charles Curran who, some years before, had spent a little time with us as a learner-producer. Although Charles was a very different man from Maurice – for one thing he was much more of a loner – he was just as staunch in his support of our work and in just as full sympathy with our general philosophy. At the time it did not enter my head that he would be the next Director-General, but when the appointment was made I had no doubts about its wisdom: the Governors had, in my view, chosen a man of unquestionable integrity, exceptional intelligence and remarkable stamina.

When we became a department my post had been redesignated Listener Research Director (L.R.D.). This title was less prestigious than Director of Listener Research would have been. Only the chiefs of the major output department were 'Directors of'. Humbler departments like Catering, Copyright, Children's Hour and mine had to be content with their functions expressed adjectively. Not long after the war D-G Haley, evidently feeling that the term Director had become devalued by over-use, restricted it to his half-dozen immediate lieutenants and re-christened the rest of us 'Heads', so I became H.L.R. I don't remember that this bothered me much but my small son's face fell when he heard about it. I suppose that 'My father is a Head at the BBC' didn't go down so well as 'My father's a BBC Director'. Years later, during one of the periodical crises in the BBC, someone was heard to mutter darkly: 'For this Assistant Heads will roll'.

2 The BBC in Labour

It may now seem extraordinary that the BBC did not set about studying its public systematically until ten years after it had become a public corporation. But when anyone suggested that it was out of touch with its public, it would point to its postbag. Listeners had not waited to be asked their opinions; they had volunteered them. From the first the BBC had been inundated with letters from listeners. There were so many, they were so varied in what they dealt with and in the views that they expressed and they seemed so manifestly authentic that few questioned their adequacy as a guide to listener opinion. A broadcaster who could triumphantly point to a pile of letters acclaiming his programme seemed to have the final answer to anyone who had the temerity to criticise it.

The seeds of doubt were sown in the BBC when it became quite apparent that the overwhelming majority of letters came from middle-class writers; that some issues – which might be called 'goat-getters' – provoked far more letters than others (reference on the air to blood-sports or the use of Bad Language were typical examples); that while many letters began 'I have never written to the BBC before', others came from people who wrote so often that they might be called BBC pen-friends had their letters been consistently friendly.

Even today there is much confused thinking, certainly not confined to broadcasting circles, about the significance of spontaneous expression of opinion. At one extreme there are those who appear to regard the post-bag as the authentic Voice of the People; at the other, those who dismiss every letter-writer as slightly mad. I know of no published study of the significance of this phenomenon – of people volunteering their views to those whom they regard as in a position to do something about it. What is its significance? What weight should be attached to it?

Every listener has an undeniable right to write and the BBC has an undeniable duty to take his letter seriously. But Programme Correspondence, as it is always called inside the BBC, has to be regarded from two quite different standpoints: as expressions of the personal opinions of the writers and as evidence of more widely held points of view. It is the failure to make this distinction which leads to confusion. As an expression of a writer's views, every letter has to be considered on its own merits. If they are pertinent and helpful so much the better, but even if they are irrelevant or misinformed (often, incidentally, more revealing of the writer than of the issue he writes about) they are welcome for they at least provide the opportunity for the BBC to state its case in reply. From this standpoint, letters from listeners are important and rightly encouraged.

The value of the post-bag as evidence of listener opinion in general is a wholly different matter. The question is not simply whether the points of view spontaneously voiced can be assumed to be shared by others who remain silent – it is a safe bet that this is always so – but rather of how widely they are shared; how many of the silent majority think the same way – is it a mere handful, a substantial group or even most of them?

But there's the rub. Granted that letters are a sample – in the sense that they are a fragment of a larger whole – the difficulty is that there can be nothing in the letters themselves to throw light on the size or nature of this larger whole. To be sure, letters often include the words 'everyone agrees with me that . . .' but this isn't evidence. In a word no one knows what any letter or bunch of letters is a sample of. It follows from this that there is no warrant whatsoever for any assumption about the extent to which the number of letters for, and the number against, some proposition indicates the relative support for these contrasting points of view amongst the general public.

This is the logical basis for scepticism about the post-bag as a reflection of wider opinion, but it does no more than show that the question is an open one. It could be argued that unless there is good reason to suppose otherwise, programme correspondence should be assumed to be representative of listener opinion. In fact there is a strong *prima facie* case for believing that it is not.

The case rests on the obvious fact that some people write to the BBC while others do not and the person who writes on one occasion does not write on another. Evidently there must be certain factors which predispose people to write. Some are obvious. People vary in extent to which they verbalise readily and in the extent to which putting pen to paper – or for that matter reaching for the telephone – is their normal method of self-expression. Some people, like the leisured and the retired, have more time for writing. People vary in their need to communicate; other things being equal it is the lonely who are the most likely to derive satisfaction from writing to the BBC. To the extent that these factors are at work they would lead to an over-representation among letter-writers of the better-educated, the more leisured and the lonely.

There must, however, be a more general factor which predisposes people to write-to-the-BBC if only because some correspondence comes from those who are not particularly literate, leisured or lonely. It is a plausible hypothesis that the compulsion to write-to-the-BBC arises when the listener feels the need to relieve his feelings – to do something which, whether or not it has any effect on the objective situation, will have the subjective effect of making him feel better. Whenever our psychological equilibrium is disturbed, however slightly, this results in some degree of unacceptable tension for which we feel a compulsion to find relief. (The tension which seeks relief may be positive or negative; it may just as well be sheer delight which cries out for expression as feelings of frustration caused by irritation or annoyance.) There are many ways by which feelings can be relieved – from kicking the cat to writing a cheque for charity – but in the broadcasting context writing-to-the-BBC is an obvious one.

To the extent that this plays a part in prompting people to write to the BBC, it means that the correspondence about a programme is *prima facie* likely to be unrepresentative of the reactions of the generality of its listeners because it will include a disproportionately large number of letters from those who, for one reason or another, felt strongly about it (quite possibly because of what they *brought* to the experience of listening rather than what the programme actually contained), and a correspondingly small number from those – quite probably a majority of the audience – who, having reacted more placidly, were consequently *not* left, when the programme ended, in a state of tension of requiring relief.

Occasionally a test case would present itself. One such was when Orwell's *1984* was shown on television in 1955. It caused a considerable furore. The BBC received an exceptionally large number of letters about it – 2,375 – virtually all of them expressing strong feelings, two-thirds protesting and one-third commending its transmission. It so happened that we had made it the subject of a questionnaire to the viewing panel so that we had evidence about the way it had been received by a reasonably representative sample of its audience. A comparison of our findings with those of the post-bag was instructive. It is true that amongst the viewing panel members protestors outnumbered commenders in a ratio similar to that of the letter-writers, but what was significant was that, taken together, these two groups were only a minority. A majority of the panel members failed to react strongly either way but their standpoint had not been represented in the post-bag at all.

If this analysis is valid it applies equally, of course, to all spontaneously expressed opinion, not merely to that directed to the BBC. Newspaper editors are well aware of this, even though 'the number of letters for and against' may be good copy; so too, it is to be hoped, are politicians. Those who cite the evidence of their post-bag as a reflection of the distribution of public opinion ('Since I raised this issue I have received hundreds of letters, virtually all supporting me') must be suspected of either naivety or cynicism.

By the time I joined the BBC its senior officials at least were treating programme correspondence, as a reflection of listener opinion, with a long spoon. But in my first few weeks I found amongst my new colleagues wide differences of opinion about audience research on each of three distinct counts: its sheer feasibility, the wisdom of the BBC's original decision to embark on it and the likely attitude of the Corporation to its findings.

On the question of feasibility, there were at one extreme those who simply refused to believe that any systematic study of the public was possible at all. They dismissed market research as so much ballyhoo; its growing use simply revealed the cynicism – or gullibility – of business men. At the other extreme were those who not merely accepted the feasibility of audience research but greatly exaggerated its potentiality. For them there seemed to be nothing which it could not do, no corner of the public mind which would not yield up its secrets to it, no problem of broadcasting which it could not illuminate.

Opinion about the BBC's decision to embark on audience research varied all the way from those who thought it an act of folly to those who thought it long overdue. The former saw it as a surrender to an ignorant clamour from a few, far from disinterested, newspapers which would not dream of taking similar medicine themselves; the Board of Governors, they argued, were the representatives not the delegates of the public and its decision to embark on audience research amounted to an abdication of its responsibilities. The latter argued that it was pure cant at once to talk of public service broadcasting or broadcasting 'in the public interest' and to refuse to set up the machinery to assess the public's views on where its interests lay. As to the likely attitude of the Powers-That-Be towards the findings of audience research, one group said (some with sorrow and others with relief) that 'nobody will take any notice of them' and another that They would alas pay them far too much attention.

I tried to avoid getting too involved in these controversies. Rather than argue about the feasibility of audience research, it seemed to me more important to demonstrate it as quickly as possible. Time alone would show whether the Corporation had been right to embark upon it and whether it would use its findings sensibly.

The most important lessons I had learnt in my years at the L.P.E. were first that there was little to be gained by trying to throw light on a dark place until someone wanted to know what was in it and, secondly, that the research worker would get precisely nowhere if he were not trusted completely. That trust could only be earned. He must be trusted not to undertake inquiries beyond the scope of the methods available, only to use methods of inquiry which he honestly believed would be effective, not to report more than he found and to be critical of his own findings.

It was also of primary importance that everyone should be clear about the role of audience research within the BBC and that I should be scrupulous to avoid exceeding it. Curiously, perhaps, this role was never specifically defined by my superiors. I had to work it out for myself and, whenever necessary, make it explicit. I can only assume that my conception of audience research's role coincided with the Corporation's for I was never called upon to amend my formulation of it.

As I saw it, it would be for audience research to gather such information about the public as was at once relevant to the needs of the BBC and susceptible of study by the methods of social research and to present this as succinctly and clearly as possible to those whom it concerned. Obviously the responsibility for defining relevance was crucial. This too was never precisely spelt out, either by me or by the Corporation. For the most part this was unnecessary for most of the matters which audience research investigated had an obvious relevance to broadcasting. But I did act on the assumption that it was audience research's duty to initiate inquiries when this seemed necessary. If these could be carried out by using existing machinery there was no problem (though there was one occasion, which will be referred to later, when this caused Displeasure). But when 'special money' was needed, a case had to be made out for it and such cases could be turned down.

In practice it was more important to lay stress on the limits of audience research's role than upon its extent. Given that it should provide information of as good a quality as it could with the resources at its disposal, disseminate it and make sure that it was properly understood, it was emphatically not part of audience research's role to apply the findings – or even to decide whether they should be applied or not; that was for those whose business it was to take action. For the BBC to have tried to insist that audience research's findings should be mandatory would, apart from making organisational nonsense, have been unworkable. Merely to announce such a policy would have created such hostility to audience research that it would soon have been frozen out. Quite apart from this, it would have been disastrous for another reason. Had audience research been involved in decision-making about matters on which it had provided information, this would inevitably have given it a vested interest in the consequences that flowed from these decisions. A research worker's only vested interest should be in the exposure of facts. So, from the very beginning of my time with the BBC, I constantly stressed that audience research's function was limited to providing the decision-makers with information upon which they could act – or not act – as seemed to them right. Map-making and navigating were quite different functions. Ours was map-making.

One had to accept the full implications of the fact that audience research was part of the BBC; created by it as a service to it. Put bluntly this meant that although its purpose was to 'seek truth', it would not be seeking truth for truth's sake but for the BBC's sake. If this had involved compromising the integrity of the work done, no self-respecting research worker would have been prepared to participate in audience research. But it did mean that in an important respect audience research in the BBC would differ from academic research.

The academic research worker expects, and is expected, to publish his findings. Not so the research worker whose job is of the nature of Intelligence for a firm or corporation. The conditions of competition alone make much market research necessarily confidential. Although the BBC was for long a monopoly, I recognised that the occasions when the findings of audience research would be fully exposed to public gaze would be likely to be relatively rare. We were frequently reproached for not publishing our findings and, with hindsight, I can see that what was called our 'secretiveness' was often unnecessary – although sometimes our failure to publish what might well have been published was merely a consequence of our having no time to spare for the administrative chores which this would have involved.

Here the basic principle of the BBC's policy was that it reserved the right to publish, or not to publish, its research findings. This was unquestionably right for if the BBC had adopted the opposite principle and conceded that all audience research findings were public property, this would in practice have crippled the usefulness of audience research. For some findings, if made public, would have been irreparably damaging to, for example, programmes still at the tender budding stage or to the careers of individual producers, artists or actors who still needed to be nursed. Moreover a policy of 'telling all' would inevitably have had highly undersirable consequences: every inquiry would have been embarked upon with one eye on the likely public reaction and the temptation to launch inquiries for no better reason than that the results were likely to reflect credit on the BBC would have been well nigh irresistible.

Some press critics argued that the public had a 'right to know' because, in the final analysis, they paid for audience research. This always seemed to me a highly dubious argument. The public's right was to a broadcasting service efficiently conducted; if the service were poor or extravagantly provided they had every justification for complaining, but the way the BBC conducted its business was its own affair.

(But though it was understood from the first that audience research findings would not be freely available to the press and public, it was equally important to preserve the principle that they should be freely available within the BBC. Hence I always tried to insist that any member of the staff had the right to see any audience research report. I saw this as essential for had the idea ever gained currency that audience research inquiries relating to a man's work were carried out without his knowledge, this would have grievously damaged confidence.)

From time to time, of course, there were leaks; audience research findings which could only have come from some source within the BBC appeared in the press. They were usually prefaced by phrases such as 'I can now disclose...' I do not recall any occasion when this caused the Corporation more than temporary embarrassment, but leaks were annoying both to the radio correspondents of rival papers – for obvious reasons – and to me because they made it more difficult to defend the policy of Open Files within the BBC. I never had reason to suspect any of my own staff of leaking information, but it was usually quite impossible to identify the culprit or the office from which the leak had occurred (in any case it was more likely to be in a bar than in an office).

The ultimate decision about whether or not to publish particular findings rested with the Head of Publicity (H.P.), acting for the Director-General. The H.P. of the day would usually consult me, but the decision was quite properly his: it had to be, for no H.P. could maintain a consistent publicity policy if individual members of staff were free to talk to the press without his knowledge. Radio correspondents, many of them I had come to know personally, would often ring me to ask for an interview or 'for a bit of information, old boy'. I was always prepared to play provided Publicity agreed that I should – and it did not take me long to be wary of an inquirer's assurance that he 'had had a word with H.P. and he had said it was O.K.'. At the same time if Publicity decided to issue a press statement based on audience research findings, or to comply with a request for information, they would consult us about its form and contents. They were well aware of how easily a layman, trying to put research findings into popular terms, can unwittingly convey the wrong impression. As often as not the man who makes 'statistics prove anything' is not so much unscrupulous as unskilled.

In deciding whether or not to publish audience research findings, the motives of the inquirer and his competence in making use of what he was given were inevitably taken into account. If Publicity were less forthcoming to press correspondents who were consistently malicious towards the BBC, who could blame them? Requests from academics engaged in research or from public bodies concerned with action in a field where the results of audience research might help (for example the Prison Commissioners interest in a report on a series of documentaries on crime) were almost invariably acceded to. Indeed in such cases we would often volunteer relevant reports.

And a clear distinction was made between the disclosure of findings and the disclosure of methods. Although the BBC's right to publish or not to publish applied to both, there was never any question of withholding information about our research methods. They were open to all and we welcomed both publicity for them and constructive criticism of them.

From time to time audience research methods were the subject of radio programmes, especially in the early years. I always enjoyed broadcasting but I did not press the case for programmes about audience research. It seemed to me that they could easily be overdone. Although there was a welcome for programmes about how the BBC worked and what went on behind the scenes, Haley, when he was Director-General, rightly pointed out that the BBC would ultimately be judged by the quality of its output. If that fell below legitimate expectations no amount of exposure of the ingenuity and skill deployed behind the scenes would cut any ice.

In this and in other ways we tried at different levels to make known the methods we used. For obvious reasons this was particularly important inside the BBC. Soon after I joined the Corporation it set up its own Staff Training School, colloquially known as St Beadle's (its first chief was Gerald Beadle). I was asked to address the first course and did so regularly thereafter. I always gladly accepted invitations to tell departmental meetings what we were up to. If individuals asked to come and put their questions personally they were welcomed even though this could take up a good deal of time. This kind of contact could be rewarding though I confess that the stream of visitors we were asked to see from overseas could be a burden. Those who were genuinely interested – and most were – could be a joy to talk to, especially if they were engaged in, or intended to start, audience research. But it was sometimes exhausting when one was faced with a visitor whose interest in the subject was peripheral, who came from a country where its application in even the remote future was hopelessly impracticable and with whom one had no common language.

Apart from the occasional broadcast, our attempts to inform those outside the Corporation's ranks about audience research methods included articles in the BBC's own and other publications, replies to letters in the press whenever opportunity arose, and addresses to gatherings from Women's Institutes to learned Societies. Some of these addresses were subsequently published.

One of such occasions was particularly memorable. This was

an invitation from its then Hon Secretary, Bradford Hill, to read a paper to the Royal Statistical Society. The prospect scared me thoroughly. My statistical training had been minimal and here would be gathered a body of men and women including some of the most eminent in this field. I took great pains in preparing my paper which had first to be submitted to two assessors. It was a relief that they let it through. The day for its delivery was in June 1944; the flying bomb campaign had just begun and the sound of their grumbling approach was still a novelty. I had just got into my stride when one was heard approaching. As the sound swelled and then ominously shut off I doubt if there was anyone in the lecture hall whose mind remained entirely concentrated on the paper being read. The reader's certainly wasn't. However none of my audience showed the slightest outward sign either of apprehension or relief when the bomb exploded somewhere else.

Many years later in the sixties the BBC started a series of monthly public Lunchtime Lectures in the Concert Hall of Broadcasting House. As they had to be strictly timed – the chairman being told to sit down at 1.15 and the lecturer at exactly 1.50 – the lecturer had to prepare a carefully timed script and read it with as much appearance of spontaneity as he could muster.

The lecturers were all senior BBC staff talking about their own specialities. It was a welcome innovation because it gave the speakers a chance to develop points at some length in the knowledge that, since they were all to be subsequently published, they were speaking for the record. The first time I gave one of these lectures was during a period – and such periods seemed to recur with the regularity of flu epidemics – when the air was thick with pronouncements about the immense power of broadcasting for good or ill. One had freedom to choose what aspect of one's work one talked about so I called mine *Reflections on the Impact of Broadcasting,* trying to point out that even the best broadcaster had to overcome considerable obstacles before he 'influenced' anybody. What I said was not, I am sure, conspicuously original, but I don't think it had been said in quite the same way before.

A year or two later the organisers of the series asked me to give another. This time I chose the occasion to talk about *The Measurement of Audiences* because the so-called 'battle' between the BBC and ITV was at its height and a lot of wholly unnecessary heat was being generated by the apparent discrepancies between the statements of each side about the way the public was dividing its time between them. I had chosen my words with even more care than usual and the paper was closely reasoned so it was disconcerting to say the least when, after I had been speaking for about ten minutes and had arrived half way down a page of script, I suddenly realised that I must have turned over two pages at once and so missed out some essential stages in the argument. One's mind moves fast on such occasions. Mine told me that the most sensible thing was to come clean. So, at the next suitable point, I said 'And now Mr Chairman I hope you and the audience will sympathise with my painful discovery that I have turned over two pages at once and will bear with me if I extemporise the missing stages in the argument.' There was a rustle of amusement but I felt I had the audience's sympathy.

It was useful to have the lunchtime lectures in booklet form to hand to people who wanted printed material about our work. But we also found it useful to prepare a brief two-page leaflet entitled 'What is Audience Research?' in which this question was answered in non-technical language. We must have distributed many thousands of them during my time.

Another kind of explanatory statement grew out of a request for a 'paper' for the BBC's General Advisory Council. At each of the Council's quarterly meetings the Corporation tabled a paper on a particular BBC activity. Its author would speak briefly to it and stand ready to answer questions. Sometimes the Council itself would specify the topic it would like dealt with, at other times the Director-General would suggest as a topic some matter on which the BBC wanted the Council's advice.

Several times during my career audience research was the chosen topic and the papers prepared, concentrating as they usually did on our methods and general philosophy, were subsequently useful for wider distribution. One of them formed the basis for the document on audience research which was submitted as evidence to the Beveridge Committee which reviewed broadcasting just after the war. The demand for reprints of papers of this kind convinced us that there was a case for producing something extensive about our methods. So we produced a printed booklet, *Methods and Services of BBC Audience Research*, in which we spelt out in some detail our function within the Corporation, how we set about our various activities and why we chose one method rather than another. This booklet had many uses. It was distributed widely within the Corporation, especially to newly joined senior programme staff; it was put into the hands of radio correspondents as background briefing; sent to other broadcasting authorities and given to any inquirers likely to take the trouble to read it. Frequently brought up-to-date, it is the answer to the charge that the BBC is secretive about the way it conducts its audience research.

I said earlier that one difference between research in the academic world and research within an organisation like the BBC is that whereas in academe one is encouraged to seek the truth for its own sake, in the world of affairs one is seeking truth for practical purposes. This has a close bearing on the question of whether and when BBC Audience Research should devote resources to studies that were primarily of wider sociological interest. A distinction needs to be drawn here between methodological and substantive studies. There was never much need for arguing the case for our conducting studies designed to lead to improvements in the methods of social research from which audience research, as part of that larger whole, would benefit, provided that it was unlikely that they would be undertaken in some seat of learning or appropriate institute (a safe bet in the early years of Audience Research). The substantive cases – those where the purpose of the study was to gather information for its own sake – often presented more difficulty. While it would clearly be impossible in good conscience to spend listeners' money on research which had no relevance whatever to broadcasting, how relevant to broadcasting must a project be in order to justify Audience Research embarking on it? And what about the cases where – and there were some, especially during the war – a problem only remotely connected with broadcasting cried out for study but only BBC Audience Research had the machinery for tackling it? In practice each case had to be considered on its merits. If undertaking a project of this kind would divert resources from projects of greater immediate relevance to broadcasting, this would clearly weigh on the contra side of the scales. Nor was it possible to give decisive weight to the understandable zeal of professional research workers to embark on the study of any problem which seemed to cry out for investigation. On the other hand we had to bear staff morale in mind and to realise that people with good research minds won't stay long in an organisation which fails to provide them with problems that stretch them.

There was always a tacit understanding that Broadcasting for Schools did not fall within Audience Research's bailiwick and I never made any attempt to question this. Schools broadcasting had a unique status; while the programmes for schools were produced and paid for by the BBC, they were commissioned by an autonomous body, the Schools Broadcasting Council. The BBC had created it and provided its funds and permanent staff but its membership consisted of representatives of the Ministry of Education, the Local Education Authorities and the teaching profession. The Council had its own team of regional Education Officers whose job it was to keep in touch with schools both by reflecting their needs and observing the reception of schools broadcasts in the classroom. Although the work which this entailed could not, and did not, claim to be research in the sense in which we understood the word, the Council were satisfied that it met their special needs and I don't doubt that it did.

The need for audience research for the External Services of the BBC did not arise until some years later. Once it did it was provided by a separate unit, quite distinct from mine. I am sure that was right not only because the administrative structures, and indeed the physical locations, of the Home and External sides of the BBC were completely distinct so that it would have been most difficult to operate any department which had to cater for them both, but also because the methods we could employ to domestic broadcasting would have been quite impracticable for external broadcasts. I greatly admired the job which the External Broadcasting Services Audience Research Officer (X.B.A.R.O.), for many years Asher Lee, did on a shoe-string for his polyglot clientele. That is a story in itself but I am not competent to tell it.

3 Sampling People

Forty years ago the practice of sampling was much less widely known than it is today. At least one respected labourer in the field of social investigation, Seebohm Rowntree, was dubious about reliance on sampling. Opinion polls, though common in the U.S.A., had hardly reached this country and the regular forecasting of General Election results was still to come. Since Audience Research would have to use social surveys based on sampling and since acceptance of their findings was bound to depend on confidence in the methods used to arrive at them, I found it necessary to seize every opportunity to explain how sampling worked and what reliance should be placed upon it.

Even though the level of sophistication about sampling is very different today, it would be a great mistake to imagine that the use of sampling in social surveys – that is surveys concerned with human behaviour, attitudes and opinions – is universally accepted, still less, understood. Today fewer people would openly pooh-pooh sampling, if only because to do so is to risk being thought an ignoramus. But even though there can be no doubt that the well-informed layman is now more common than he was, there can also be no doubt that there are now more half-informed laymen and this carries with it its own dangers – that too much will be expected of sampling and the method discredited whenever such expectations are disappointed.

This chapter is therefore an attempt to come to grips with the major kinds of scepticism still sometimes encountered and the kind of misunderstandings with which I had to contend. There was one kind of sceptic who for some time baffled me. Dispose of his objections one by one and his antagonism only became more intense. Confront him with undeniable evidence that sampling worked and he just didn't want to know. It was obvious that his reactions were emotional, and strongly so. Could it be, I wondered, that his obscurantism arose from fear? Suppose he had some article of faith so deeply based that any threat to it was intolerable and suppose he suspected that were he to admit the validity of sampling in social inquiries this cherished belief would be undermined. This would be enough to account for the vehemence of his resistance to persuasion. In such a case further rational argument would be useless; the only hope would lie in discovering what this article of faith was and then showing him, if one could, that his fear that it was threatened was groundless.

The more I thought about this, the more sure I became that the cherished article of faith must be that man is a creature capable of reflective thought, free to make conscious choices. From this flows the feeling which we all share, even those who suffer most from a sense of their own inferiority, that in the final analysis each of us is unique as a person. Since this is a faith which men in our society live by even, I suspect, those who claim to be determinist, it is inevitably defended tenaciously.

But sampling is based on the predicate that conclusions about large populations can be inferred from data about a limited number of them. This could be the nigger-in-the-wood pile, for if it be true, it might seem to imply that men are merely replicas of one another and so to conflict with the idea that each man is unique. Worse still, if sampling facilitates conclusions which enable man's behaviour to be predicted, what becomes of man's capacity to choose how he will act?

The nigger-in-the-wood pile deserves a close look. What kinds of conclusion about populations can be inferred from studying limited numbers of them? Conclusions about their physical characteristics certainly, about their heights, weights, blood-groups or their life-expectancy. Significantly, no one is upset by the use of sampling to provide these kinds of data. This is presumably because we are under no illusions about man being autonomous in these areas. We enjoy no exemption from the laws which govern the material world – such as gravitation – and are as subject to decay and death as any other organism. It is only to the application of sampling to the area of personality that objections are raised because it is only in this area that free will can have any meaning; it is only *as persons* that we can exercise choice and it is only *as a person* that each of us feels himself to be, and maybe each of us is, unique.

In one important respect the conclusions arrived at when sampling is applied to the field of the personal are similar to those derived from its application to man in the physical and organic fields: they too relate to particular characteristics, attributes or aspects of men and not to men as such. A man's ability to perceive relationships, the strength of his attachment to his family or football club or the tenacity of his prejudices are as much characteristics of his personality as his rate of metabolism or blood-count are characteristics of him as a living organism or his height and weight are characteristics of his body. (The fact that personality characteristics are much more difficult to measure quantitatively is irrelevant.)

Once this point is grasped much of the apprehension we are discussing will be seen to be groundless. For our feeling of uniqueness is not that we are unique in each of all our many characteristics, but that we are unique *as persons*. As persons we are more than the sum of our characteristics; personality is a dynamic relationship of an individual with his environment. Thus my feeling of personal uniqueness is not threatened if it should turn out that I share the same interest in gardening as the man next door or that there are fifty other men in my neighbourhood who react in exactly the same was as I do to high-pressure salesmanship. These findings would disturb me no more than if it were shown that my ability to withstand cold were identical with that of half the other men of my age. Multiply the particular respects in which I am not unique a thousand times and still my uniqueness *as a person* can remain inviolate.

What of the fear that, because the social scientist's study of people reveals that they behave predictably (and hence that sampling is a reliable tool of investigation), this must imply that individuals have no real freedom of choice but in reality are mere automata? This too is based on a misunderstanding. It is the notorious 'no-one-has-ever-asked-me' syndrome. One often hears it said that 'If the results of that sample survey claim to show what I think (or feel or do), it must be wrong because I have never been questioned'. But the fact is that no such claim is ever made. It would be impossible for any sample survey to pronounce upon the opinion or behaviour of any specific individual from whom it did not obtain evidence precisely because men are free and can, if they wish, choose not to conform to type. What a sample survey can do – and all that in most cases it is intended to do – is to predict what particular types of people are likely to be thinking, feeling or doing or are likely to think, feel or do should the same circumstances recur.

To take a hypothetical case: it might well be possible, as a result of a properly conducted social survey, to tell a *Times*-reading 60-year-old consultant physician, who had never heard that a survey had been made, that he was ten times as likely to disapprove of the National Health Service, and three times as likely to vote Conservative as his *Daily Mirror*-reading 30-year-old chauffeur. These would be legitimate statements of probability. But no sample survey, no matter how large and well-conceived, could ever say with certainty what his, or his chauffeur's, attitudes to the National Health Service or voting intentions are because both are free men, at liberty to conform or to be mavericks as they choose.

It was my experience that once the issue was put in this light what I have called the emotional reaction to the sampling of people tended to subside and the way was left clear for rational explanations of other perplexities. Some of my colleagues, though willing enough to accept my assurance that it could yield reliable descriptions of large populations, would profess to find this entirely mysterious. I was never happy to leave it at that for I felt that their confidence would be far more securely based if they could see why sampling was a valid and reliable procedure.

First it was necessary to point out that though a sample was indeed no more than a fragment of a whole (or 'universe') that did not mean that any fragment would do. To be a valid sample it had to be selected in such a way as to be a miniature, a scale-model, of the universe. That small scale models could efficiently represent large physical objects like bridges or buildings was, of course, a matter of common experience. What then remained to be explained were the procedures for selecting samples for social surveys and the *a priori* grounds for believing that they would yield samples which could claim validity.

Two selection procedures are now commonly in use – sometimes in combination. One is known as Probability Sampling, the other as Quota Sampling, although, when Audience Research began, Quota Sampling was in almost universal use and was frequently referred to as Random Sampling – a term which has since fallen into disuse. The essential principle behind both procedures is that, ideally, each individual member of the population to be studied must have an exactly equal chance of being selected as a member of the sample. Any departure from this ideal will inevitably distort the sample. Thus if a sample of school children is to be drawn and the selection procedure gives children of above-average intelligence a greater chance of being selected than children of below-average intelligence, then the sample eventually selected will to that extent be biased.

Probability Sampling seeks to achieve this ideal by adopting a method of picking the sample which entirely eliminates the human element from the actual process of selection. Typically, every *n*th name is chosen from a complete list of the names of the entire population, *n* being determined by dividing the population by the size of the sample required; (thus if the population numbers 100,000 and a sample of 1,000 is required, *n* will be 100). The human element is even excluded from the decision about which should be the first name to be picked.

This is truly selection at random and strictly only samples selected in this way are entitled to claim that they are Random Samples. I frequently found, however, that to refer to selection 'at random' was a stumbling block to understanding. Random sounded too much like uncontrolled, haphazard or even casual, whereas, in fact, it is none of these. Perhaps 'deliberately random' might have been a more accurate description. Be that as it may, I frequently had to make it clear that the purpose of Random Sampling was to ensure that the choice was determined by chance, and by chance alone.

'That is all very well', the sceptic might answer, 'of course I can see the importance of eliminating the human element from the selection of the sample – because that could easily bias the sample – but what is there to stop deliberately random selection from throwing up a sample which bears little or no likeness to the population? How can you be so sure that, if you leave the choice to chance, the resulting sample will be valid, i.e. will be truly representative?'.

It is not entirely frivolous to reply, as the phlegmatic tourist did when told by an enthusiastic Canadian of the staggering tonnage of water which hourly flowed over Niagra, 'Well What's to stop it?'. For leaving the choice of the individuals who will constitute the sample to chance alone implies the elimination of all other determinants including any which could promote the candidature of some indviduals over that of others. It means, in a word, equalising the chances of all. From this it logically follows that, of all the possible samples which *could* emerge from random selection, the one *most likely* to emerge is the one which exactly mirrors the population. Of course the desired end – the representativeness of the sample – is not an either/or affair; it is a matter of degree. In practice it is improbable that a sample drawn at random will turn out to be an absolutely exact miniature of the population, but the odds are heavily in favour of such a sample being a close approximation to it.

Anyone can test this for himself. Let him put a quantity of marbles of differing colours – say 100 of each red, blue, green, yellow and orange – into a cylindrical tin and rotate it several times so that they are all thoroughly mixed up. Then, without looking, let him take out twenty and record the number of each colour amongst them. If he repeats this process five times he will have selected five different samples, by a process in which chance alone will have determined the number of marbles of each colour. Whilst it is quite likely that none of his five twenties will consist of equal numbers of marbles of each colour, it is highly probable that, with each successive drawing, the cumulative total will have come near to this, so that by the time a hundred have been drawn out there will be fairly close to twenty of each colour.

If he has the patience, let him replace the abstracted marbles and repeat the process – adding the results to those he obtained the first time. And let him repeat it several times if he wishes. It can be said with certainty that the more he does so the closer the numbers of abstracted marbles of each colour will approach equality and thus reflect the composition of the total population of marbles which he put in in the first place.

The other selection procedure, Quota Sampling, is sometimes used in combination with Probability Sampling. In its pure form it is less than ideal because it does not entirely eliminate the human element in selection. But it does reduce it very drastically, some would say to the point where it is no longer of serious consequence. And there are circumstances in which Quota Sampling has to be used because Probability Sampling is impracticable.

The essential difference between Quota and Probability Sampling is that whereas in Probability Sampling the proper composition of the sample, i.e. the right numbers of different kinds of people, can confidently be left to emerge automatically, in Quota Sampling the composition of the sample is prescribed in advance, at what might be called the drawing-board stage.

The first step in Quota Sampling is therefore the assembly of whatever statistical information is available about the population to be studied. To take a very simple example, if there were to be a survey of the television viewing habits of 12–18 year-old school children in a London borough, the available information about this population might look like this:

	%		%		%
Boys	49	At Comprehensive Schools	50	aged 12–14	55
Girls	51	,, Grammar Schools	18	15 or 16	30
	100	,, Secy. Modern Schools	29	17 & over	15
		Other	3		100
			100		

D

Suppose it had been decided that the sample should number 500, administrative arrangements then have to be made to ensure that the sample should be distributed in these proportions. (A Probability Sample would have thrown up these distributions automatically.)

If the survey were to be carried out by interviewers calling at private homes this would mean fixing a quota for each interviewer (hence Quota Sampling). The interviewers' quotas need not all be the same, provided that, when they are aggregated, they mirror the shape of the population. Thus one particular interviewer, from whom a total of twenty-five interviews was required, might be instructed to distribute them thus:

Attending:	Aged 12–14		Aged 15 & 16		Aged 17 & 18		Total
	Boys	Girls	Boys	Girls	Boys	Girls	
Comprehensive Schools	2	4	2	2	–	2	12
Grammar Schools	1	1	1	1	1	–	5
Secondary Mod. Schools	3	2	1	1	–	–	7
Other kinds of school	–	–	–	–	1	–	1
	6	7	4	4	2	2	25

The interviewer would have to fulfil these quota requirements, and persevere until she had done so, but the distinctive feature of Quota Sampling, and where it differs fundamentally from Probability Sampling, is that she could fill her quotas by interviewing *any* two 12–14 year-old comprehensive school boys, *any* four comprehensive schoolgirls of the same age group, *any* grammar school boy or *any* grammar school girl aged 12–14, and so on.

There is, of course, no denying that this leaves the door open for the human element to affect the selection of the sample, but in practice there are several factors which can usually be counted on to militate against its ill effects. First, the area within which personal bias could exercise a distorting influence in strictly limited by the quota system itself. It could not, in the example given, prevent the sample from being a microcosm of the population in terms of sex, age, area and type-of-school because these are givens. Secondly, many interviewers will be taking part in the survey and there is at least comparative safety in numbers. If one interviewer has a bias towards, say, the studious-looking child this may well be counteracted by another interviewer's bias towards the more rumbustious children. (This incidentally is a strong argument in favour of employing many interviewers to do a modest number of interviews each rather than giving a heavy load to a few.)

Thirdly, there are ways in which interviewers can be encouraged to set about their work which discourage an exercise of personal bias and may at the same time make their task both easier and more efficient. For instance, they can be recommended to call systematically from house to house and take what comes. In this way a particular quota – say that of the one grammar school girl of 17 or 18 in the example – will automatically be filled by the *first* such girl whom the interviewer encounters.

These, then, are the two methods of sampling in use in social surveys. It is probably easier for the non-mathematically minded layman to see the logic behind Quota Sampling, for an understanding and an acceptance of Probability Sampling does demand some familiarity with the laws of probability.

There was a time in the late forties when the protagonists of Probability Sampling in social surveys, developed in Professor Rensis Likert's Survey Research Centre in the University of Michigan, and the protagonists of Quota Sampling, under the Gallup banner, argued endlessly and tediously about their relative merits at every international conference or whenever two or three were gathered together. But the argument, thanks to some solid studies comparing the results obtained by the two methods, is now mercifully stilled. It is generally agreed that the Probability method is preferable when it is practicable but that when it cannot be used the Quota method, if handled skilfully and intelligently, can produce results of which no one need be ashamed.

Other perplexities about sampling had their source in the

innumeracy common among highly literate men. For example, I was asked again and again how big a sample should be. This frequently went along with a conviction that a sample which was small, in relation to the population it represented, was *ipso facto* suspect. I would be asked whether I regarded a sample numbering a hundred (or fifty or two hundred or whatever) as reliable, or I would hear people say: 'How can this sample, numbering only five hundred, possibly tell you anything when it is supposed to represent a population of twenty million? It's only one in forty thousand!'

In trying to deal with these questions I would first have to get people to realise that a sample's reliability, like almost everything else except pregnancy, is a matter of degree. Strictly, therefore, the question 'Is a sample numbering x reliable?' is, like 'Have you left off beating your wife?', not susceptible of a Yes or No answer. The appropriate question is 'How reliable is a sample numbering x?' Even then there must be a mutually accepted definition of 'reliable'. Statements about the reliability of samples take this form: given a sample numbering x, there is a two-to-one chance (or a nineteen to one chance, or it is virtually certain) that a given finding will be accurate to within plus or minus so-and-so. For instance if, out of a sample numbering 400, eighty people were found to be living in semi-detached houses, then the chances would be 19:1 that dwellers in semi-detached houses accounted for between 16 and 24 per cent of the population from which the sample was drawn. (Most people will accept 19:1 odds as reasonable in these circumstances.)

There are standard tables, based on the laws of probability, showing the accuracy which can be obtained by using samples of different sizes. The important thing they reveal is that, although it is true that the bigger the sample the greater its accuracy, increasing the sample's size does not bring a commensurate increase in its accuracy. The Law of Diminishing Returns is at work. Taking our study of the incidence of semi-detached houses as an example, it was said that, with a sample of 400, there was a 19:1 chance that our finding would be accurate to within 4 per cent each way. But if we had arrived at the same finding with twice as big a sample we should only have reduced the margin of uncertaincy from 4 to about 3 per cent. Furthermore, if we had wanted to reduce it to 1 per cent, our sample would have had to have been increased to 6,000.

Bearing in mind that the cost of conducting social surveys is, apart from overheads, directly proportionate to the size of the sample, this is a very strong deterrant to blythe increases in sample size.

It will probably have been noticed that the calculations above take no account of the magnitude of the population from which the sample is drawn. This is because, surprisingly perhaps, the size of the population plays no part in determining the sample's reliability. If a well-conducted survey, based on a sample consisting of 500 of City *P's* population, revealed that 30 per cent of them had bank accounts, the odds would be 19:1 that the true figure lay between 26 and 34 per cent – and these limits would apply no matter what the total population of City *P* was. The answer would be the same whether it were 5,000, 50,000 or half a million.

At first sight this may seem contrary to common sense but in fact common sense confirms it. Somerset Maugham once said 'I do not have to eat a whole sheep in order to know what mutton tastes like; I only have to eat one chop – *but I must eat that*'. An analytical chemist, seeking to test the purity of a river's water at a particular point in its course, does not need to vary the size of his sample according to the size of the river: a beaker-full will be enough however much water is flowing by. The chemist has, of course, other things to worry about, such as being sure not to take his beaker-full from a stagnant backwater. In short it is not the relationship between the volume of his sample and the volume of water in the river which matters, but how representative his sample is.

To be sure, sample-size is important not only because the larger it is the more precise its findings will be but also because the larger it is the greater the opportunity for deriving more information about the population by examining sub-sections of the sample. But what is called the 'sampling ratio' – the number of people in the population divided by the number in the sample – can be ignored because it is irrelevant to the sample's reliability.

It is, of course, true that surveys based on sampling can go wrong, but when they do it is always because something has gone wrong with its execution and not because the principle is at fault. The most notorious cases are those of opinion pollsters wrongly forecasting election results. (The glee with which their discomforture is greeted is a measure of the emotional resistance to the application of sampling to people.) In fact the election pollsters successes far exceed their failures – indeed it is because their failures are so rare that they have news-value – but it is worth looking at some of the reasons why they may fail.

The most obvious is that the steps taken to ensure that the sample should be unbiassed were just not good enough. It was this which accounted for the conspicuous failure of *The Literary Digest* to predict the winner of the 1932 U.S. Presidential election. Despite an enormous sample it predicted a victory for the Republican candidate, Thomas Dewey, whereas with a miniscule sample Gallup correctly predicted the election of Franklin Roosevelt, the Democrat. The trouble lay in the *Literary Digest's* sample, which was limited to telephone subscribers. That hadn't mattered in previous elections because they had divided, as between Republican and Democratic, in much the same way as had the electorate as a whole, but it did matter in the 1932 election – in the middle of the depression – for then the division of opinion was much more conservative v. liberal than it had previously been, and as telephone subscribers, being better-off, tended to be conservative whereas the rest of the population tended to be liberal, they were no longer an unbiassed sample.

One of the inevitable hazards which beset election pollsters is what to do with the 'Don't Knows'. If their numbers are substantial and support for two of the candidates is nicely balanced, then the way in which the 'Don't Knows' eventually vote (if they vote) may be decisive. Having counted the declared voting intentions of his sample, the pollster must make some estimate of the intentions of the 'Don't Knows' before he produces any forecast of the election result. Some pollsters are better at this than others, but in any event this part of the process has nothing to do with sampling and, if it goes wrong, the process of sampling can't be blamed.

The same can be said of another hazard the election forecaster faces – the possibility that people will change their minds about the way they will vote between the time they were questioned and election day. All that can justifiably be claimed for the results of a well-conducted poll is that it reveals how the electorate would have been likely to vote had the election taken place on the day they were questioned. To use these data to predict how the election will eventually go involves making assumptions about the extent to which, and the directions in which, voters will change their minds and not vote as they said they would. This, again, is a matter of judgement, which may, or may not, be skilful, but it has nothing to do with the sampling process. In the famous case of the U.S. Presidential Election of 1948, when the pollsters (and the pundits) confidently but wrongly forecast a defeat for Harry Truman, it seems more than likely that their forecasts were belied because there was in fact a last-minute swing in favour of Truman sufficient to enable his opponent to snatch defeat from the jaws of victory.

Personally I was always thankful that I was not involved in election forecasting, if for no other reason than that the criterion of success is an excessively exacting one – an either/or affair – and the penalties of failure are out of all proportion to its deserts. This calls for some explanation. As has already been explained, in a normal social survey the findings are expressed in terms of probability: that on given odds the incidence of some event is likely to lie between certain specified limits – depending on the size of the sample. Where the survey concerns the comparative incidence of two events it may well be that it has to say that they occur with something like equal frequency but that the size of the sample makes it impossible to say which has the edge over the other. Such a finding is not a failure – the discovery that the two events do occur with approximately equal frequency may well be all that anyone needs to know.

But in election forecasting a miss is as good as a mile. The election forecaster is understandably reluctant to announce that his sample only allows him to say that either Candidate *A* or Candidate *B* may win – that their supporters are so nearly equal in numbers that it is a toss-up. He is expected to say which one will win and, if he gets the answer wrong, woe betide him; he will get no sympathy if he pleads that his findings showed that either might win, but that he happened to put his money on the wrong one.

To sum up, I had to persuade some of my colleagues that it is a complete misconception to think that the use of sampling to discover facts about people implies that people are mere 'things', as interchangeable as ball-bearings. The successful application of sampling to human problems has no relevance to the free-will/determinism controversy and the fact that sampling facilitates accurate predictions about the behaviour of groups of people has no bearing whatsoever on the question of whether people are, or are not, free agents.

Others had to be persuaded that there is no mystery about the efficacy of sampling. Provided that the selection of the sample is unbiassed, the laws of chance can safely be left to ensure that it will be a microcosm of the population from which it is drawn. Indeed the ideal method of sampling – the Probability method – derives its virtue from its rigorous exclusion from the selection process of everything but chance. The Quota method is second best only because it is less rigorous in excluding the human element from the selection process.

It had to be frequently reiterated that the reliability of a sample was not a matter of either/or but was one of degree. The notion that there was such a thing as a right size for a sample, regardless of the purpose which the sample had to serve, was one which died hard. The right size, in any given case, depended on the extent to which viable sub-divisions of the sample were needed and the degree of precision which was required of the findings. A quite small sample would serve if it were not to be sub-divided and if an answer within plus or minus 10 per cent of the truth were good enough, but if many sub-divisions were needed, each yielding findings of a very high degree of accuracy, the sample might have to run to many thousands. (At the same time one would point out that whereas the cost of sampling rose in direct proportion to any increase in the sample's size the rewards, in terms of greater precision, certainly did not.)

The misconception that a small sample of a large population was *ipso facto* unreliable (or that a large sample must be all right simply because it was large) was equally persistent, perhaps because it seemed such plain common sense. In reality it is common nonsense. If it were true then, before a pathologist took a blood sample, he would first have to weigh the patient.

4 First Fruits

When Tallents' Listener Research Committee first met we found ourselves in full agreement about tactics. There had been quite enough talking about audience research already so the sooner we had something tangible to show the better. We thought it wise to display a becoming modesty in setting our sights. I suggested that for three reasons radio drama would be a suitable field for our first experiment: I already had an ally in Val Gielgud, it was a type of output which had a wide following, and it so happened that I was personally better informed about it than about some other types of broadcasting.

My plan was to see if it were possible to provide the Drama Department with a regular flow of information about how its plays and features were regarded by those who chose to listen to them. It was to be primarily an experiment in method; if the methods we used provided useful information for the Drama Department so much the better, if they did not we should at least have learnt how not to do it.

How should we gather the information? We would be seeking to reflect the views of those who had actually listened to specific plays and features. Ideally we should have liked to have interviewed them soon after the event, but this was out of the question with the resources then available. They would have to be sent questionnaires by post. But who should we send our questionnaires to? How many should we send and how many could we expect back? Above all, how valid would the answers be?

I recommended that we should set up what we should call a Drama Panel, to run for three months. It should consist of ordinary listeners whose one essential qualification should be a taste for plays and features. We would send them all a questionnaire about each production and invite them to complete

First Fruits 59

and return it if, but only if, they happened to listen to it in the ordinary way – with return postage prepaid.

The questionnaires would each be tailor-made. The questions would all be such as any reasonably intelligent lay listener could answer. Alternative answers should be provided as often as possible, though with space in which the more loquacious could spread themselves. We also laid plans to see whether people would have to be rewarded for taking part in the exercise.

We had to accept that at this time there was not the remotest possibility of using orthodox sampling methods to recruit the panel. This meant that we would not be able to demonstrate that the views we collected reflected those of the actual audiences; although we would of course be sensible about selecting our panel, in the final analysis the most we would be able to report was what the listeners who had answered out questions had said. But this would be better than nothing. So on the principle of not letting the best be an enemy of the good, we went ahead.

We recruited a panel of 350 listeners. Most of them were suggested by BBC colleagues (such as Regional P.R.O.'s and Education Officers) who came into frequent contact with the public, some were people who had written to the BBC about its drama and others were people who volunteered to help when they read in the press that a Drama Panel was to be set up.

We did our best to persuade panel members to resist the temptation to listen to plays for no other reason than that they had received questionnaires about them. And this was a temptation, at any rate at first. Answering a questionnaire could, some of them said, be an interesting exercise in itself. (Moreover it probably induced a forgivable feeling of self-importance.) But it was important to the success of the enterprise that this temptation should be resisted. Since what we were seeking was contact with representatives of the 'real' audiences who would have listened even if the Panel hadn't existed, it followed that anyone who listened to a play solely in order to answer our questionnaire was *ipso facto* an intruder. And so not only in this first experiment, but also in all the inquiries of a similar kind in the years that followed 'No Duty-Listening Please' was a recurrent injunction.

Over those experimental months forty-seven productions were the subject of questionnaires. The plays ranged from *Anthony and Cleopatra, All for Love* and *The Cherry Orchard,* to *Dear Brutus* and *East Lynne.* The features have titles now long forgotten, but they had such titles as *The Battle of Lepanto, The Blue Danube, King Arthur* and *The First Days of Steam.* In the questionnaires we tried to distinguish between the theme, the production and the performance. The results showed, incidentally, that the standard of both production and performance was either invariably very high or else that panel members were very uncritical of them, for in these respects few differences between the broadcasts emerged. In fact such differences as there were showed a suspiciously close correlation with the differences in the way the themes were regarded – the more a play's theme was liked, the more highly was its production and performance regarded – an example, no doubt, of the 'halo effect'.

Our primary concern with method was of less interest to the Features and Drama producers than the reports on individual productions. Till then they had no evidence of public reaction other than that of their personal friends and letters from listeners. (Press criticism was, of course, a different kettle of fish.) Often this evidence was sparse and contradictory. Now, for the first time, there was something substantial and systematic, admittedly with weaknesses, but an earnest of what might be done. At least it showed that there were ordinary listeners who would co-operate and answer questionnaires.

Among the methodological lessons we learnt was that rewards for co-operating and staying the course were unnecessary. For example, the level of co-operation obtained from a group who were offered complimentary copies of the *Radio Times* and *The Listener* during their membership was no higher than that of a control group who were offered no reward at all. Another lesson was that the most effective form of question was one for which both a set of alternative (cross-out) answers and a 'space for comment' were provided. Offering alternative answers – even if one of them had to be 'not sure' – ensured that evidence was obtained from virtually all those returning the questionnaire (and in a form highly convenient for tabulation). Giving the panel members the opportunity to add comments in his own words reduced the danger of irritating those who felt that none of the alternatives offered quite fitted their case. It also often provided insight into what really lay behind the 'cross-out' answers. Of course since by no means all those answering the questionnaires availed themselves of the opportunity to comment, it would have been improper to have treated what was said by those who did as a reflection of the views of the whole group. Any statistical tabulation of 'free comment' had therefore to be kept carefully apart from the tabulations of 'alternative answers'.

The final report on the experiment brought a note of congratulation from Reith, gracious in view of his earlier misgivings about starting up audience research. Besides gathering the threads together, the report looked ahead. It reviewed the needs of each of the main output departments in turn – Features and Drama, Variety, Talks, Outside Broadcasts and Music. Among its conclusions was that in some cases the primary need was for some way of measuring the size of their audiences, in other words for providing broadcasting with a substitute for the 'box office'. With hindsight it can be said that the most remarkable thing about this recommendation was its date, 25th June, 1937, for that was only nine months after Audience Research began when any suggestion of measuring the size of audiences would have been regarded as almost indecent. Now not only could it be discussed but a proposal that it should be tried actually received the Corporation's blessing.

A description of the first 'box office' experiment will be found in the next chapter. To keep the record straight, something must first be said about another, quite different, kind of experiment which was launched soon after the Drama Panel had been wound up. Both the Drama Panel and the proposed 'box office' involved studying the impact of broadcasts after they had been transmitted. But it was clear that there was also a need for 'background information' which would not necessarily relate to specific programmes. Facts about the public's living habits – who could listen when – were the most obvious example. (At that time there were still senior officials in the BBC who found it hard to believe anyone dined before 8.00 p.m.) The collection of such data would not have to be continuous, for habits change relatively slowly; periodic studies would meet the case. There would be no difficulty about formulating the necessary questions nor about getting listeners to answer them; the problem would be to ensure that the answers came from people who, collectively, could be taken as representative of the public as a whole.

There were two suggestions which were clearly non-starters. Both were obvious though this did not prevent them from being repeatedly put forward in the years to come as brilliantly original. One was that an issue of the *Radio Times* should include a questionnaire which all its readers should be asked to answer. This would certainly be a cheap method of distribution and indeed would have other virtues if the sole object were to collect a large volume of replies. But it clearly would not do where it was essential that the replies should demonstrably represent the listening public. Although the immense circulation of the *Radio Times* was the pride of the BBC, in fact it only reached one listening family in three. A plan which relied on *Radio Times* readers' co-operation would thus begin by disenfranchising the majority of the listening public. Moreover it was inconceivable that, however many readers played ball, they would be more than a minority and the problem of deciding how far those who had replied were representative of those who had not would require exactly the same kind of survey as that for which putting the questionnaire in the *Radio Times* was suggested as a substitute.

The second proposal was that everyone buying a wireless licence should be handed a questionnaire to complete. If this had been adopted as it stood, the BBC would have lain itself open to the rather daunting possibility of coping with up to eight million completed questionnaires a year. But, pace the pirates, the GPO's files of wireless licence-holders certainly did constitute a unique listing of the names and addresses of listening households. If we wanted access to a sample of them here was the perfect source. So we decided to see if they could in practice be used. The GPO agreed to instruct local offices to address envelopes to licence-holders selected according to our instructions. For our part, we first selected, at random, a number of postal districts, and then we worked out a formula for drawing samples from each of the selected district's licence files so as to yield a total of 3,000 licence-holders. As we wanted questionnaires to be completed not only by the person who took out the licence but also by all members of the family over the age of 16 and as, of course, we did not know how large the family of each licence-payer was, we sent each of them three extra copies for the use of other members of his family (and an invitation to ask for more if required). Three was the chosen number because we knew this would be enough for the vast majority of families. A reply-paid envelope was enclosed in each packet.

The questionnaire was an austere single foolscap sheet for we had to make do with what the BBC's internal duplicating service could provide. D(despatch) – day was early in January 1938. Completed forms came back from 44 per cent of the households approached. At the time we thought that this was not too bad, although it still was not good enough. But we were gratified that the total number of completed questionnaires was 3,152 for this was an average of 2.4 from each household. Since the size of the average family (excluding children) was 2.7, this meant that the vast majority of the licence-holders who had co-operated must have got all the other adults in his household to do so too.

We made a very careful analysis of the nature of the response, comparing its composition with that of the listening public where we knew this or, failing that, of the population as a whole. We found that the sex-, age- and regional-composition of the returned questionnaires closely resembled those of the population. The response had a distinct middle-class bias, but as we did not know at that time how far the listening public itself had a middle-class bias, we were in no position to say whether this was at all excessive.

All this was encouraging but, of course, there was no gain-saying that 56 per cent of those approached had *not* responded. Something must have deterred them, but what was it? And whatever it was, did it render the 44 per cent who had co-operated unrepresentative? If those who did not co-operate were simply not sufficiently interested in the enterprise, was his insufficient interest in answering a questionnaire or in radio-listening, or both? But whatever the answer, the crucial issue was the extent to which refraining from co-operating was related to the issues about which questions had been asked.

Common sense suggested that sometimes it was and sometimes it wasn't. It seemed unlikely, for example, that the working hours of the non-cooperating 56 per cent would have differed from those of the co-operating 44 per cent. On the other hand the same could certainly not be said of a question about the frequency with which some series of radio programmes were listened to, for if one reason for returning the questionnaire was an interest in radio, then the answers of the 44 per cent would be likely to show an a-typically high frequency of listening.

The inquiry had quite limited objectives, and the choice of the things about which questions were asked is an interesting reflection on what was preoccupying the BBC planners at that time. There were questions seeking to find out when, if at all, people listened in the day-time (defined as between 8.00 a.m. and 6.00 p.m.) and what kinds of programmes they liked to hear then. Others asked about when listening usually started and stopped in the evening and there were questions about the frequency of listening to specific news bulletins, the *Sports Bulletin*, the *Topical Talk* (which at that time came after the 10.00 p.m. News) and one other series, *American Commentary* (then given weekly by Raymond Gram Swing at 9.20 each Saturday night).

The results suggested that day-time listening rose to a peak between 1.00 and 2.00 p.m. After a decline it rose again in the afternoon to reach a second peak between 5.00 and 6.00 p.m. Around midday the overwhelming majority wanted to hear light music of some kind – indeed there was very little demand for anything else at this hour. There was a substantial demand for variety, plays and talks in the later afternoon. But few wanted day-time radio to include either orchestral and choral music, vocal and instrumental recitals, or chamber music.

Most of those who listened in the evening either switched on or were already listening, at 6.00 p.m. (The 'nobody-dines-before-8' brigade were staggered to learn that most people had finished their evening meal before 7.00 p.m.) The listening audience did not diminish appreciably until 10.00 p.m. but thereafter it rapidly faded away, except on Saturday nights.

The *6 o'clock News* was the one with the largest following, nearly 60 per cent said they always or nearly always heard it; the *Second News* (which was at 7.00 p.m.) had comparatively few listeners but 33 per cent said they regularly heard the *Third News* (at 9.00 p.m.) and 21 per cent the *News Summary* at 10.00 p.m. 14 per cent said they were regular listeners to the *Topical Talk* and 16 per cent to the *Sports Bulletin*. 12 per cent said they always or nearly always listened to Raymond Gram Swing.

There was a second similar experiment six months later, in the summer of 1938. This time questionnaires were completed by 12,700 people living in the households of 4,700 licence-holders. The proportion of licence-holders co-operating was smaller than in the winter, 35 per cent instead of 44 per cent, but the degree of co-operation from the families sending forms back was higher; the average number per family being 2.6 instead of 2.4 (out of a possible 2.7).

The questionnaire for the second experiment looked far more attractive – we had even managed to persuade the BBC to let us employ a layout man. There were more questions about listening habits, designed to enable us to see how far these were different in summer time. There was also a question 'for those who like grand opera' asking whether they would like more (or less) from Covent Garden, Sadlers Wells, Glyndebourne, 'abroad' and 'the studio'.

But the whole of one side of the foolscap questionnaire was headed 'What do you like?' Twenty-one types of programme were listed and listeners were invited to put a X against the kinds he liked. Elsewhere there was 'space for remarks'. This was the first of a number of attempts we made during my time at the BBC to carry out a census of what we came to call 'tastes'. (For convenience we confined the term 'tastes' to attitudes towards broad categories of output as distinct from particular broadcasts. Similarly we used the word 'reactions' to refer to the way people felt about specific broadcasts which they had heard or viewed.)

Sociologists will recognise the measurements of listeners' tastes as an example of attitude measurement, 'attitudes' being roughly defined as 'dispositions'. The measurement of tastes in broadcasting is a notoriously tricky business. In the first place the choice of the right terms to describe the various different categories of output presents acute problems. Obviously the descriptive terms used should be free from ambiguity; they must mean the same thing to all. If such descriptions as Military Bands, Grand Opera or Cricket Commentaries cause little trouble, others certainly do. Demarcation disputes were frequent even within the BBC. Was a *Scrapbook* the proper concern of the Variety Department or of Features and Drama? We all thought we knew what a Feature was, but could we expect ordinary listeners to do so? They might hear them and like them but still not recognise them under this title. (And one could hardly blame them for the word was used quite differently in the film world.) Or take 'Talks': this term was certainly in wide use but it covered so heterogenous a field – from the reminiscences of elderly yokels to philosophers discoursing on the Meaning of Meaning – that two listeners could say they 'liked talks' and yet have in mind quite different kinds of material. Music presented another kind of difficulty. We knew we should have to represent music by several categories and we suspected (and we were right) that the pertinent sub-divisions were not so much different kinds, but different levels, of music. We could, of course, have listed 'Serious Music', 'Middle-Brow Music' and 'Light Music', but how could we be sure that such terms meant the same thing to everybody? (Some time later we discovered that *In a Monastery Garden* was considered by many people as an example of serious music.) In this first inquiry into tastes we compromised, listing separately Orchestral Music, Piano Recitals, Violin Recitals, Vocal Recitals, Chamber Music, Grand Opera, Light Opera and Operettas, Light Music, Brass Bands, Military Bands and finally Theatre and Cinema Organs.

The way in which the question should be posed – or rather the way in which we would ask that it should be answered –

presented a quite different kind of problem. Tastes, like all attitudes, are matters of degree. If a man is asked whether or not he likes X, a 'Yes' may mean anything from enthusiastic affirmation to half-hearted assent. (And incidentally in these circumstances some of those without strong feelings are likely to answer 'Yes' simply because this is more socially acceptable than saying 'No'.) The obvious way of grappling with this difficulty is to offer a scale of alternative answers ranging from, say, 'I like it very much indeed', through 'I have no strong feelings', to 'I strongly dislike it'. But if the object of the exercise is to compare people's attitudes towards different things, even this does not fully solve the problem. A man who chose the reply 'like very much indeed' when asked to express his feelings towards his neighbour and subsequently chose the same reply when asked about his wife could not therefore be said to like them equally. His two answers would not be comparable because he would have applied different standards, liking his neighbour 'very much indeed' *as a neighbour* and his wife 'very much indeed' in the rather more exacting role of spouse.

But there is no denying that 'yes/no' answers are much easier to present. The researcher is always under pressure to simplify the statement of his findings. The layman much prefers a statement that simply says that '80 per cent like X while only 60 per cent like Y', to one which says that 'though 80 per cent like X, this includes only 30 per cent who like it very much, the rest, 50 per cent, liking it moderately. On the other hand though only 60 per cent like Y, 40 per cent like it very much and only 20 per cent like it moderately.'

There is, of course, a simple way in which graduated replies can be condensed for presentation. By giving a numerical 'weight' to each position on the scale, such as $+2$ points for each like-very-much answer down to -2 points for each dislike-strongly, the answers can be shown as a single figure – the number of points scored. This indeed is frequently done, although the choice of the weight given to each position on the scale is crucial. It is often based on arbitrary assumptions about the right relationship of the various answers. It may not in practice be any the worse on that account, but if it is felt necessary to establish scientifically what the weights should be, this can involve very expensive and time-consuming preliminary research. And there is one disadvantage in using 'scores'; because they are abstract, it is far harder for the layman to grasp their significance than that of concrete statements such as that 20 per cent of the population likes this and 40 per cent likes that. We were not unaware of these problems back in 1938 but nevertheless we decided to grasp the nettle and go for the simplest method, believing that the Corporation was not at that stage ready for anything more sophisticated.

In barest total terms the proportions saying they 'liked' the twenty-four categories of output emerged as follows:

	%		%
Variety	93	Cricket Commentary	48
Theatre and Cinema Organs	82	Serial Plays	47
		Light Opera and Operettas	38
Military Bands	72		
Musical Comedy	69	Vocal Recitals	32
Dance Music	68	Tennis Commentaries	26
Plays	68	Piano Recitals	21
Light Music	66	Grand Opera	21
Orchestral Music	55	Violin Recitals	19
Brass Bands	55	Serial Readings	12
Talks	53	Chamber Music	8
Discussions	49		

Listeners' free comments showed, not surprisingly, that there was sometimes confusion about the meaning of certain of these categories. The report notes 'an appreciable number of listeners took Orchestral Music to refer to light orchestral music and some of the votes for both Piano and Violin Recitals ought probably to have gone to Light Music'.

The object of the exercise was as much to provide data about the nature of the public for each category as to compare the size of the publics for different categories. The report compared the voting of men with that of women, of middle-class and working-class listeners ('class' being based on the stated occupation of the heads of the household), of listeners in different age groups, of listeners in different sizes of family, of urban and rural listeners and listeners in different BBC regions.

The voting of men and women differed remarkably little, the one outstanding exception being Cricket Commentaries which were 'liked' by 66 per cent of men but by only 30 per cent of women. A significant difference between the voting of middle- and working-class listeners was that whereas the middle-class listeners 'liked' an average of 10.2 of the categories, working-class listeners 'liked' 9.8, though we never knew whether this meant that middle-class listeners were more catholic in their tastes or simply more inclined to say 'Yes'. Middle-class listeners gave more of their votes than did working-class listeners to Talks and Discussions, Orchestral and Light Music, Grand and Light Opera, Recitals and Tennis Commentaries (these were the days of 'Anyone for tennis?'). On the other hand working-class voting was heavier than that of the middle-class for Variety, Theatre and Cinema Organs, Military and Brass Bands, Musical Comedy, Dance Music and Serial Plays. There was little difference in respect of Plays, Cricket Commentaries, Vocal Recitals or Serial Readings.

Age proved to be a sharp discriminator. Light Music, Plays, Serial Plays, Tennis Commentaries and most of all Dance Music declined in popularity with each step up the age scale. Nine out of ten 16–20 years-olds said they liked Dance Music as compared with less than three out of ten over-70s. Talks and Discussions, on the other hand, showed the reverse tendency. Talks, for example, were liked by three out of ten 16–20 year-olds and six out of ten over-70s.

The smaller the family, the more likely were its members to vote for the more demanding types of programme, for example, 14 per cent of those who lived alone said they liked Chamber Music and 28 per cent of them that they like Grand Opera, but the corresponding figures for those in families of five or more were only 5 per cent and 16 per cent respectively.

The tastes of rural and urban listeners differed remarkably little. Regional differences, too, were less than some people expected but the Welsh and the Scots voted more heavily than the English or the Irish for Vocal Recitals, while listeners in the North, as was expected, showed a special partiality for Brass Bands and Scottish listeners were less interested in Cricket

Commentaries than were listeners in the rest of Great Britain.

Aside from whether the quality of the data in this early study was all that it should have been, of what real use is information of this kind? The old hands were, of course, quick to declare that they knew it all already. Up to a point they were right. Everyone knew that far more people would say they liked Variety than would say they liked Chamber Music, but by no means everyone would have predicted that men's and women's preferences were as similar as they proved to be. Besides, the ranks of the old hands were getting thinner, their places were being taken by younger men and women who preferred facts to folk-lore. But even if this study had little use *per se*, that was not the end of the matter. We saw it as merely the first of a series, much of the value of which would come from comparisons. Was it true, as was so often said at that time, that broadcasting would 'raise public tastes'? A series of inquiries on these lines should, we thought, contribute to the eventual finding of an answer.

In the years which followed we did in fact conduct a number of inquiries into the public's tastes. The results of one formed part of the evidence supplied to the Beveridge Committee in 1948 and a later one appeared in *The Public and the Programmes* (BBC Publications, 1958). The sampling methods were improved, eventually attaining a very high degree of validity; the categorisation of output was refined, though some of its problems remained intractable, and the actual questions asked became a good deal more sophisticated than those we used in 1938. To some extent these improvements, desirable in themselves, made it rather more difficult to draw comparisons over time, nevertheless there could be no denying that the similarities in the findings of successive surveys were far more striking than the differences between them. So much was this so that it was difficult to resist the conclusion that, broadly speaking, the tastes of the population didn't change – or at any rate that if there were changes they escaped detection by these methods of inquiry.

This is not to say, of course, that there were not individuals whose tastes changed. Such changes, which might result from the experiences of listening or simply the fact that the individual was getting older, could take place without affecting the picture for the population as a whole. Thus today's enthusiasts for Opera may include many who had no time for it ten years ago, but if they have done no more than replace those who have died, or lost their enthusiasm, since the last count, the taste for Opera *amongst the population as a whole* would have remained the same. (One never sees the same river twice.)

But the pioneers of broadcasting hoped for more than this. By making the best available they looked to broadcasting to widen cultural interests; to increase the proportion of the population who derived pleasure from the best music, the best drama, the best poetry and the best ideas. These successive inquiries, covering more than three decades, produced no convincing evidence that this hope was being fulfilled. Moreover similar surveys in different countries within the Western world all produced remarkably similar results. This suggested that basic tastes for the kinds of material with which broadcasting could deal were anything but mercurial, being far less susceptible of change than had been expected, perhaps because these tastes are grounded in the cultural environment of the society in which people find themselves and as such are as resistant to modification as are all value-systems first formed during the years when the individual is growing to maturity.

The readers of the first tastes report had to be explicitly warned that 'audiences' could not be predicted from findings of this kind. The number of people who would actually listen to any particular broadcast of a given kind could not be inferred from the number of people who had said they liked the kind of output of which it was an example. To have established the size of the public for, say, Musical Comedies, did not bring us any nearer knowing how big the audience for a particular musical comedy broadcast would be. For any of a number of reasons a listener who had expressed a taste for musical comedy might fail to hear it – he might be out that night; be in but prefer to read a book, or have to defer to someone else's choice; he might not know it was 'on'; have known it was, but have forgotten or he might have failed to have listened to it because, though he usually liked musical comedy, this was one he did not care for.

Nor was there any reason to suppose that for every category of output the relationship between the size of its 'public' and the size of its typical audience would be the same. Different categories of output might well vary in what might be called their 'rate of turnover'. For example, it might well be that the 'turnover' of Variety's public was much less than that of, say, Plays: that the proportion of the Variety public which could be counted on to listen to Saturday *Music Hall* was much higher than the proportion of the drama public which could be counted on to listen to *Saturday Night Theatre*. (This is certainly true of the printed word. In the course of a single week the proportion of Proust fans who actually read *Remembrance of Time Past* is likely to be a good deal less than the proportion of Fleming fans who actually read a James Bond.) In short, whatever measure of success we had achieved in identifying and analysing the publics for different kinds of output, the problem of audience measurement still remained to be solved.

5 Numbering the People

By the mid-thirties several methods of measuring the size of radio audiences were in use in the U.S.A., but they had grown up in response to a need which did not exist in Great Britain. Virtually all radio was commercial there, American stations deriving all their income from selling time to advertisers who would fill it with 'sponsored' programmes in the course of which they would promote their wares. Naturally the stations' space-salesmen had to be armed with information about the audiences they could 'deliver' to the sponsors. It was soon found that advertisers were not satisfied with vague statements about the number of people who habitually listened to a station. They demanded information about the number of people – and the kinds of people – who actually listened to it on specific occasions. And they wanted this not only because it was a better guide to the value of what they were asked to buy but because, once they had bought time, it would show them whether in fact they had bought what they hoped they had. These measurements of audiences became known as 'ratings' – rather unfortunately for the word 'rating' could equally well describe measurements of other kinds, such as of audience enjoyment or comprehension.

The three main methods then in use in the U.S.A. were the 'simultaneous telephone call', the 'meter-method' and the 'recall' method. It wasn't until many years later – in the early sixties – that a method to end all methods was devised. It was the product of a Mid-Western University. Its inventor declared it to be 'An instrument to provide permanent film records of dynamic situations'. Automatic cameras which would switch themselves on when required (and could not be tampered with) would be installed in a sample of viewing homes. They would faithfully record everything which happened within visual range of the TV receiver for as long as this was switched on. There would be no worries about informant veracity; the camera could not lie. Its creator had tested it out. He had already installed it in nearly a hundred homes and reported fascinating results. As his exposition said: 'Every conceivable kind of activity goes on in front of a TV screen, eating and drinking are the two most commonly found, but many persons combine TV watching with card-playing, games playing, sewing, working out cross-word puzzles, allegedly studying, fighting and making love.' But why, we wondered, had it been called the Dyna-Foto-Chron? Would not Big Brother have been shorter? It must be sadly recorded that, as far as is known, no broadcasting organisation, commercial or public service took it up.

The 'simultaneous telephone call' method was the most widely used before the war and its principal practitioner was C. E. Hooper Inc. Hooper operated in the major cities of the United States; he selected samples from telephone directories and phoned them, asking them to say which station, if any, their radio was tuned to at the time the phone rang. He produced what he called a Hooperating for each show, i.e. the number of homes in which the show had been switched on expressed as a percentage of the number of homes telephoned.

One obvious criticism of this method was that it could only provide information about homes which had telephones. Hooper maintained, however, and with some plausibility, that homes without phones were so few in the United States that their exclusion didn't matter. Another criticism was that he could only give a Hooperating for each show *as a whole*. This did not satisfy advertisers who suspected that their audiences might well fluctuate *during* shows. What mattered most to them was how many homes had heard the 'commercials'. Further, there was a limit to the American public's tolerance; it did not go so far as to welcome telephone calls late at night or early in the morning so there were parts of the broadcasting day for which no Hooperating could be provided. But Hooper's virtue lay in the elimination of the memory factor for the caller was asked about what was happening 'now', not about what 'had happened'. In this respect he had the advantage over those who used telephone calls to get people to recall their listening over the past few hours.

Those who offered a 'recall' method sometimes gathered their data by personal interviews on the doorstep. This, they pointed out, enabled them to include non-telephone homes in their sample. Others asked people by telephone to recall their listening. Either way their costs were far lower than Hooper's since they gathered so much more information at each interview than he did. Their services were therefore widely patronised by the less affluent stations and advertisers.

But the big challenge to Hooper came from Neilson. Art Neilson, a Swedish-American, was a perfectionist. By training an engineer who had already built up in Chicago a formidable market research business, C. A. Neilson Inc., he was convinced that some mechanical way of measuring radio audiences must be possible. He knew, of course, that the record of domestic electricity consumption would be useless for it could not discriminate between listening to different stations or even between radio listening and an outburst of ironing by the housewives of America. Devising a mechanical method of measuring radio listening was therefore a challenge to him. With a remorseless energy he poured vast funds into the development and promotion of the Neilson Audimeter. Even though by any other than American standards the cost of his service was prodigious, the inevitable eventually happened; C. E. Hooper Inc. 'folded' and Neilson reigned supreme.

Fitted to the back of a radio receiver, the audimeter would automatically trace, on a moving coil of time-calibrated tape, a continuous record of the stations to which the receiver had been tuned. Neilson installed meters in a sample of homes and collected the tapes at weekly intervals. His end-product was the Neilson-rating. There could be Neilson-ratings for each station for each moment of the broadcasting day, each showing the proportion of the homes in the sample which had been tuned in to it.

The advantages which Neilson claimed over Hooper were that his sample was superior because it was not confined to telephone homes; that the human element was entirely eliminated and above all that he could produce, as Hooper could not, measurements relating to the precise moments when commercials were on the air. Neilson's system was not however free from disadvantages. He had to persuade householders to allow him to install his meters and it was not to be expected that everyone would consent. His critics were quick to point out that unless listening habits in the homes of those refusing to cooperate were the same as those in the homes of those who did, his results would be biassed. (It was suspected that there would be less listening in the homes which rejected Neilson's blandishments.)

Furthermore Neilson's meters could, at best, only record the behaviour of receivers, not that of people. To the extent that sets were left switched on even though no one was listening to them, the Neilson-rating presented a false picture. Neilson brushed this objection aside as of negligible importance. But there was a more cogent objection arising from the fact that Neilson-ratings did not relate to people but only to households and the numbers of individuals listening per set-in-use notoriously varied very widely from one broadcast to another. Thus two shows might have had equal 'audiences', in terms of households-tuned-in, but if one had been listened to by an average of three people per household and the other by only 1.5, then the latter's audience, in terms of numbers of individuals, would have only been half as big. Hooper overcame this difficulty by getting his telephone girls to ask how many people were listening to the show the receiver was tuned to, but Neilson's meters were no help to him here. The only thing he could do was to supplement his meters by getting his sample families to keep diaries of their listening, recording the number of people in the household who were present when the set was on: an expedient which, whatever might be said for it, could lay no claim to the virtues of being mechanical.

The problem of conducting audience measurement in the United States differed greatly from that in any other part of the world because of the multiplicity of their radio stations. Many cities were served by as many as a dozen and no two cities were alike. (Ostensibly this offered listeners a wider choice but to European ears the choice was somewhat illusory. The stations all being in competition with one another, most of them were hell-bent on securing the largest audiences. This frequently meant that to switch from one to another was merely to move from one comedy show to another.)

The demand for audience measurement was, of course, far less clamant in countries served by non-commercial broadcasting. They had no advertisers to satisfy or persuade to buy time. There was also far less demand for moment-to-moment audience measurement for this mainly derived for the need to know how many people heard the commercials. In the context of public service broadcasting the need for audience measurement came mainly from the programme planners' concern to assess the effect, in terms of consumption, of the pattern of broadcasting they had devised. The programme planner in the public service system was not primarily concerned to maximise the number of listeners. Where there was only one station within his control his greatest concern was to see that the different ingredients at his disposal had a fair crack of the whip so that music lovers, sports fans, the drama public, and those who only wanted good clean fun, would get a fair share of broadcasting time at periods when they could listen. If he had more than one outlet at his disposal, his planning task was of course that much easier. But in either case he did not think of the population he served as a single monolithic mass but as a number of different 'publics' – some small, some large and often overlapping – a public for plays, a public for light entertainment, a public for sport, a public for symphony concerts, another for dance music and so on.

It was this kind of thinking that led us to think departmentally in our own first attempt at audience measurement. The department we chose for our first experiment was Variety (now called Light Entertainment). Our sights were not set on establishing the absolute number of listeners to each show but rather on determining the relationship between them. For that reason we decided to recruit our sample from amongst the 'variety public' – the people who were in the market for this type of output. We decided that we would try to get a thousand of them to form a panel required, over a limited period, to tell us which of the various variety shows broadcast they had listened to.

The first step was to recruit volunteers. The kernel of the campaign was to be a broadcast appeal, backed up by publicity in the *Radio Times* and a press handout. The broadcaster was John Watt, a genial round-faced show business character who had recently been elevated from producer to Director of Variety. So at the end of *Music Hall* on Saturday, 18th September, 1937, he took over the microphone and engagingly explained, in quite simple terms, what we wanted and why we wanted it: that the volunteers would only have to note down the shows they had heard, and that it would be made easy because we would supply them with weekly lists, that the postage would be paid and that the job was to gather information that would help the BBC to give them a better service.

The response startled us. We received 28,000 postcards, listing 47,000 listeners who were prepared to help.

The following Saturday John went on the air again to thank the volunteers and tell them that it would be impossible to accept all the offers but that, in view of the magnitude of the response, the BBC had decided to be doubly ambitious and enrol two, instead of one, thousand.

The empanelled 2,000 were chosen at random (every twenty-third name) so that we could be sure that they represented the entire 47,000 who had volunteered. We should have liked to have been able to compare the composition of the chosen 2,000 with that of the variety public but at that time we did not know how this was composed. The best we could do was to compare it with the composition of the population as a whole. Their sex distribution was 57 per cent male and 43 per cent female as compared with 48 per cent and 52 per cent for the population. The volunteers were slightly younger than the population as a whole, their median age being in the 30s whereas that of the population was in the 40s, and they had a slight middle-class bias (45 per cent of them were middle class whereas our estimate was that 40 per cent of the population was middle class as we then defined it). In geographical terms the South-East was over-represented among the volunteers, the Midlands and the North were somewhat under-represented and the Celtic fringe quite markedly so. (This paralleled my experience in advertising. Every analysis of the 'coupon response' to advertisements showed the same pattern – even when the coupon included an offer of a free sample.)

Of course this still left open the crucial question: to what extent would the information we should obtain about the volunteers' listening to variety programmes parallel that of the variety public as a whole? We arranged to set up a Control group to throw some light on this – but more of that later.

We christened the scheme The Variety Listening Barometer, for it was to measure pressure rather than heat, and the participating volunteers were called log-keepers. They were enrolled for a twelve-week stint running from the beginning of October to the end of the year. Each week they were sent a Log, listing the forthcoming week's variety programmes of which there were usually about thirty-five (significantly there were none on Sundays). They were invited to answer three questions about each one: 'How much of this did you hear?' 'Did you start listening after it had begun?' and 'Did you stop listening before it had finished?' (These questions were in fact unnecessarily elaborate. Had we simply asked 'Did you listen to this?' we should have arrived at substantially the same conclusions.)

'Please do not feel', we said in the preliminary guide, 'you must make a special effort to listen because you are keeping a log. What we want is a record of ordinary listening. Therefore please listen just as much or as little as you would have done if you had never heard of this scheme. Remember we are just as interested to know which programmes you did *not* hear as which ones you did.' We also stressed that it was the logkeepers' own listening we wanted to know about, not that of his family, and we suggested that he should 'mark (the log) every day or two rather than leave it until just before you have to send it back'.

We knew full well that, in asking people to record what they were listening to, we were asking them to perform a less congenial task than that of saying whether or not they had enjoyed what they had heard. Saying what you think is much more fun than recording what you do. So we decided to carry out a test. We divided the log-keepers into two, similarly constituted, groups, 'A' and 'B'. The 'A' group was asked to refrain from writing any programme comment on the log-sheets themselves; if they wanted to comment they should use a separate sheet of paper. The 'B' group was invited to comment 'on the back of the form', which was obviously easier. If there were a lower rate of return of log-sheets from the 'A' group this would suggest that the discouragement to write comments was a disincentive to co-operate. In fact the 'A' group responded so well that there was no room for the 'B' group to do better. From both groups we were still receiving 92 per cent of the weekly logs back when the experiment ended.

In another experiment we tested the comparative effect on the staying power of the log-keepers of requiring them to return their logs at weekly, fortnightly and monthly intervals. There proved to be virtually no difference. 87 per cent of those who had to return them at the end of each week, and the same proportion of those who had to return them fortnightly, were still doing so in week twelve, while 92 per cent of those who had only to return them monthly stayed the full course.

As the findings began to appear what the producers were most interested in was, of course, the comparative magnitude of the audiences for their own shows. The names of some of these shows will evoke memories. Typical findings were that 83 per cent of the log-keepers listened to the average *Music Hall* or *Palace of Varieties*, 72 per cent to *Monday Night at Seven*, 68 per cent to *Caroll Levis and his Discoveries* and 60 per cent to the average studio variety show. Lunchtime light entertainment would be listened to by 24 per cent of them. Dance bands, such as Henry Hall's, late in the evening would draw 47 per cent. But the *Royal Command Performance* topped them all with 94 per cent.

But for the planners it was not only the audiences for particular shows that mattered but the more general inferences such as that Saturday variety audiences were half as large again as those on Tuesday-Friday with Monday coming between; that more people listened to the National than to the Regional Programme, as the two networks were then called, or the differences between the compositions of the audiences for various categories of light entertainment – Vaudeville, Comedy shows, 'Rough Funny Shows' as John Watt called them, 'Interest' programmes like *In Town Tonight,* American relays and so on.

To assist the planners further we sent to log-keepers, in addition to their 'logs', occasional questionnaires on various policy points. For example, we asked for preferences as between 8.00–9.00 p.m. and 9.20–10.20 p.m. for Saturday night *Music Hall,* (8.00 to 9.00 p.m. was preferred by a 2 : 1 majority); whether 6.30 p.m. on Fridays would be a convenient time to listen to light entertainment and whether this would be better than the same hour on another day (it was); and how late people were prepared to listen to light entertainment (half had gone to bed by 10.30 p.m. on weekdays and by 11.00 p.m. on Saturdays).

We decided to test the representativeness of the panel's listening by getting logs completed by a Control Group – a sample of listeners who had *not* volunteered to help us nor, as far as we knew, were other than normal in their partiality for light entertainment. By today's standards the selection of this Control group was crude, but it was the best we could do. We went personally to friendly employers – such as a departmental store, a printing works, a Civil Service Department – and obtained permission to go round their premises asking their staff to log their previous week's Variety programme listening on the spot. At least they had no idea we were coming. (The 'we' were myself and my small departmental staff in London and some colleagues on the regions.) We did the job in two sample weeks. In the first we interviewed twelve hundred people and in the second, a month later, another fifteen hundred. Besides asking them which programmes they had heard, we also recorded their ages and occupations. We all found it a tiring but rather exhilarating exercise. Personally I do not remember anyone refusing to answer, though many were at first mystified. One problem was to convince those who said they 'didn't listen much' that their fears that they 'wouldn't be any use to us' were misconceived: they found it hard to understand that negative replies were just as important to us as positive. And it was sometimes a problem to disengage oneself tactfully from a too time-consuming explanation.

In terms of sex, social class and regional distribution this Control group tallied reasonably well with the panel – which was a relief. When we compared the listening of the Control group with that of the panel two highly significant facts emerged. The first was that the Control group listened to variety programmes far less than the panel did. (The average programme's audience included 37 per cent of the panel but only 22 per cent of the Control group.) The second was that this relationship was pretty constant from programme to programme. The order in which the programmes fell was much the same whether it was determined by the magnitude of the panel member audiences or those of the Control group audiences. Put statistically, the coefficients of correlation between the two orders were $+0.89$ for the first week tested and $+0.79$ for the second. (Had the two orders been exactly the same the coefficient would have been $+1.00$ and had they been the reverse of one another it would have been -1.00.)

The first of these findings – that the log-keepers would listen more to variety than would the Controls – was expected, though we could not have forecast precisely how much more omnivorous the log-keepers would be. It was expected not only because the log-keepers, unlike the Control group, were deliberately drawn from the ranks of the variety public, but also because they had volunteered to do the job whereas the Control group had been more or less bounced into it. Moreover we felt sure that, despite all our efforts to discourage them, some of the log-keepers had listened simply because they were keeping logs.

The second finding – that from programme to programme Control Group listening proved to be a pretty consistent fraction of log-keeper listening – had far-reaching implications for audience research for it bore upon the problem of what is known as volunteer-bias, i.e. the extent to which people who volunteer to take part in a piece of research are *ipso facto* untypical of the general population in respects which relate to the subject of the inquiry. (Nobody minds volunteers being untypical in irrelevant respects.)

If, as we hoped, the log-keepers differed from the Control group only in that they consisted of volunteers with a known penchant for listening to light entertainment, then it would follow that any differences between their listening and that of the Control group would be a measure of their a-typicality. In terms of the *quantity* of listening, the log-keepers were clearly highly a-typical, but in terms of their *selection* of programmes they were not. Assuming the Control group to be representative of the general population, then the conclusion to which this pointed was a highly practical one: that, while data supplied by volunteers provided an unsatisfactory basis for inferring the *absolute* quantity of the general public's listening programme by programme, it could be a reasonable guide to its *relative* quantity. We could not deduce the number of listeners to programmes P and Q from such data but we could deduce from them the relationship between the sizes of these audiences. Volunteer listening would differ substantially from that of the general public *in degree*, but it would not differ much *in kind*. The picture of the pattern of listening which was based on volunteer evidence would, in a word, be an exaggeration of the general public's listening, but not a gross distortion of it. Since at this stage in our history the chances of our being able to afford to dispense with the volunteer system were remote, this was a highly encouraging conclusion.

But the reasoning could be carried further, for it also had an application to the use of volunteers for ascertaining listeners' reactions to programmes – what they thought of the programmes they listened to. We asked ourselves why it should be that the log-keepers showed so little volunteer-bias in their selection of programmes. Of course we knew that a listener's expectation of enjoying a programme was only one of the factors determining whether he would listen to it. He might fail to do so because he could not be home in time, because his wife wanted to hear something else or because his children were making too much noise. He might listen to it merely in deference to somebody else's wishes or because he could not bother to switch the set off. But there was no *prima facie* reason to suppose that these extraneous factors, many of which were in any case beyond the listener's control, affected volunteers any more, or any less, than they affected the rest of the population.

That left Expectation for consideration as a factor in the decision process. If log-keepers' expectations of the various programmes had differed from those of the Control group, there would have been a low correlation (or even a negative one) between the orders in which their listening, and that of the Control group, placed the programmes. But the two orders were very much the same. So the implication was that, even though the volunteer log-keepers had an abnormal appetite for light entertainment, they liked much the same things as everyone else. This reassured us about using volunteers' views of the generality of listeners. This conclusion was, of course, tentative but in want of better we based our future policy upon it, taking every opportunity to test it in the years that followed. I still believe it to be basically sound.

The Variety Listening Barometer was certainly a breakthrough. Within a very short time the BBC agreed that the principle should be extended to programmes in general. Volunteers had again to be used, for the days when we could conduct a survey based on personal interviews were still to come, and it was clearly understood that we would be estimating no more than the relative audiences of programmes.

This time 4,000 listeners were 'empanelled' for a four-month period of duty to produce what was called the General Listening Barometer. The logs were greatly simplified – the log-keeper only had to say whether he had or had not listened to each programme. We had learnt too, that unless we could produce the results hard on the heels of the broadcasts' transmission they would hardly be worth having as a practical aid. So punch-card machinery was installed and it was a source of wonder and delight within the BBC. A stream of colleagues dropped in to see elegant young women operators – the first the BBC had ever employed – tapping keys which transformed logs carefully marked up by listeners into patterns of holes on cards and to watch with wide-eyed wonder the punched cards flutter through a counter-sorter at what then seemed an incredible speed, each mysteriously selecting its appropriate hopper. And this was only thirty-odd years ago.

By now audience research had ceased to be a novelty. I had been joined by Bobby Cockburn as my deputy and had a staff of half a dozen. The Listener Research Committee had ceased to meet – I think Tallents was satisfied that we would not do anything silly – and our relationships with other departments were harmonious. As well as the major experiments which have been described we were undertaking a number of *ad hoc* studies of a modest kind. These included the first study of the impact of television (the Television Service had begun in 1936). The number of viewers was still very small and confined to London (it was even possible to invite them all to a tea-party at Alexandra Palace). But in those days viewers were so fascinated to see anything on their screens, and producers so beset with the problem of getting programmes on the air at all, that there was little useful we could do.

One of our experiments proved a total failure. Few music critics devoted much of their space to broadcasting so we thought – and the Music Department agreed with us – that something might be done to encourage knowledgeable listeners to contribute a regular flow of informed criticism of broadcast performances. A number were therefore invited, and readily agreed, to form a Rosta of Music Critics. But their observations proved so diffuse and so contradictory that our plan had to be abandoned in despair. The Rosta sank without trace.

Among the BBC's overseas offices news of the activities of audience research was of particular interest in New York, where Felix Greene was in charge. He reported that in the United States interest in the possibilities of audience research had spread beyond commercial and professional broadcasting circles to the academic sociologists and psychologists. The Rockefeller Foundation was financing a Radio Research Project at Princeton University. An old friend of mine, Paul Lazarsfeld (a psychologist of the Viennese school) was involved and so was the late Professor Hadley Cantril. Felix, a cousin of Sir Hugh Greene, and later to become famous as a friend of the Chinese People's Republic in the days when this was regarded as almost indecent, suggested that the BBC should send me to America to see what was going on and to meet my opposite numbers in the radio networks.

This was my first visit to North America. I crossed by sea in January 1939 and when I arrived I found Felix full of the news that in a few weeks he would be off to London on the first regular trans-Atlantic passenger flight in a heavier-than-air machine. Like everyone else I found New York exhilarating.

In the dry, cold sunshine one's step seemed lighter and one's energy greater than in damp London.

The research men on the two great networks, Mal Beville of NBC and Frank Stanton of CBS (later to become its President) welcomed me with a generous cordiality which I soon learnt was characteristic of America. I went to Princeton and saw the set-up of the Radio Research Project, to Chicago to meet, among others, the legendary Neilson, to Toronto to establish friendly relations with the Canadian Broadcasting Corporation which in many respects had been modelled on the BBC.

But time was running out; every day one became more conscious of the approaching long shadow of war. For me, as for many others, as the thirties drew to their close it became harder to shake off the feeling that our professional lives – to say nothing of our private lives – were under suspended sentence. The catastrophies piled up, the re-occupation of the Rhineland, the rape of Abyssinia, the Spanish Civil War, Germany's grim descent into barbarism, the forced *Anschluss*, then Munich. When we witnessed the occupation of Czechoslovakia we knew that war was only a matter of time.

On the day that Hitler marched into Prague I was dining with Raymond Gram Swing whose voice was well known in Britain from his weekly *American Commentary*. He was a passionate democrat and the kindliest of men, yet as the news came through he said almost with exultation in his voice: 'This makes war inevitable.' Since I, like he, had felt humiliated by Munich, perhaps I should logically have shared his mood. But I didn't.

The day I landed at Southampton Mussolini occupied Albania. One could almost hear the shutters of Europe coming down but until the inevitable happened one had to carry on as though it still might not and during the last few months of peace we went on planning with a growing sense of futility. The General Listening Barometer had worked well while I had been away so it was decided to make it a permanency – to start, significantly enough, in September 1939.

6 Audience Research in War-time—I

Most of us expected that London would be subjected to a devasting aerial bombardment within minutes of a declaration of war. One had to force one's mind to imagine what life would be like for the survivors. Would they be more than a few blind men groping for food? The BBC had made plans to evacuate staff to various parts of the country to maintain essential services. In the last months of peace a mysterious character called the Defence Officer had been appointed and I did not envy him his chilling job. It seemed futile, and even frivolous, to imagine Audience Research could have any role in the kind of world that would be left. So I was not surprised when we were told that we were in Category B which meant that on the declaration of war we were to remain at home to await orders (if, one thought, there would be anyone left to give or receive them).

In the event, of course, a week after the declaration of war London was miraculously still there and we began to adjust ourselves to what turned out to be a winter of 'phoney war'. Within a few days I was summoned back to lend a hand with the flood of correspondence which had soon started up. There was plenty for people to write about. The infant Television Service had closed down for the duration and the National and Regional radio networks had been replaced overnight by a single BBC Home Service. To begin with it transmitted little but news and gramophone records though it soon included a full range of programmes.

For most people, of course, its most important ingredient was *The News*. But there wasn't much news and listeners were soon complaining bitterly that they heard the same news over and over again – which, of course, they would do if, as many of them did, they listened to every bulletin. Some thought it deplorable that in a time of war the BBC should broadcast anything 'frivolous', others that its programmes were too solemn, that more should be done to 'keep people's spirits up'. Reading these letters I got the impression that many people were feeling as though they had stepped on a stair which wasn't there and were taking it out on the BBC.

As it was impossible to judge how far these letters represented the views of the silent majority, there was a job for Audience Research to do. Within a few weeks I had brought the rest of my staff back and we organized a rushed, but useful, inquiry about the impact of the BBC Home Service on the public in general.

The programme planners found themselves very much at sea. There had been considerable shifts in population; many children had been evacuated and an unknown number of families had left the big cities for safer areas. Places of entertainment were shut. The blackout was keeping people at home in the evenings and would do so increasingly as the winter approached. So it was decided that Audience Research should conduct a social survey to try to establish some new landmarks.

Since it would be essential that the findings should be quantitatively reliable, it was agreed that it should be based on personal interviews with a substantial sample. At that time we had no facilities for conducting the fieldwork of such a survey so I commissioned my old friend Mark Abrams at the London Press Exchange to do it for us. The survey took place in October 1939, the sample consisting of 3,500 homes spread all over Great Britain. Information was collected about everyone living in these homes at the time: who they were, what their working hours were and so on.

Meantime the D-G. (Reith had by this time been succeeded by Sir Frederick Ogilvie) asked me to prepare a long-term plan for audience research in war-time. My recommendation was that we should set ourselves two aims: to measure the amount of listening which was taking place and to reflect public opinion about broadcasting. To achieve these aims we should set up two pieces of machinery: a Continuous Survey of Listening and a network of Local Correspondents.

The object of the Survey would be to estimate the actual number of listeners to each programme, not merely their relative sizes as we had previously done. The data would therefore have to be gathered by personal interviews with samples of the population; reliance on volunteers, working through the post, would no longer be good enough.

But we should still rely on volunteers to man the other piece of machinery. We could, I suggested, keep in touch with public opinion about broadcasting by recruiting as Honorary Local Correspondents a large number of the kinds of people who, because of the jobs they did or the roles they performed, might be expected to be in touch with local feeling. They might be shopkeepers, milkmen or publicans, for example, or parsons, WVS workers or perhaps Air-Raid wardens. There would be nothing secret about their activities, indeed there would be much to be said for their being known as Honorary Local Correspondents of the BBC through whom suggestions and complaints might be easily passed on to us.

This two-tiered plan was accepted and by December 1939 the Continuous Survey of Listening had begun. It has continued ever since though greatly enlarged and now, of course, known as the Survey of Listening and Viewing. It was, and still is, based on two principles: first, that the population's listening (or viewing) can be inferred as accurately as is in practice necessary from that of a properly designed sample; second, that the sample's listening can be discovered by reminding them of the programmes that they could have heard and asking them which ones they actually did listen to.

The rationale lying behind the first of these principles is discussed in Chapter 3 which those to whom it is familiar may thankfully have skipped. Behind the second lay assumptions about people's memories of what they had listened to and their readiness to disclose this to interviewers. The memory-factor was relevant because it would have been quite out of the question – on cost grounds – for us to have used methods, like the 'simultaneous interview', which would have made no demands on memory at all. What we had to decide was how far back in time we dared go. We had no doubt that some broadcasts would be a great deal more memorable than others. For example, anyone who had heard it would be unlikely to forget Chamberlain's broadcast to the nation announcing the outbreak of the war or, in happier times, the outside broadcast from the Spithead Review at the time of the Coronation in 1937 from which the world learned that it was not only the Fleet which was lit-up. On the other hand anyone could be forgiven for quickly forgetting a broadcast of café music to which they had listened as a background only a few hours before.

But since our task was to construct as accurate a picture as possible of the quantity of listening to each and every broadcast every day, the interval between the act of recalling and the event recalled would have to be such as to allow listening to the least memorable broadcast to be recalled accurately. We had, as it were, to use a net with a mesh close enough to trap the most elusive fish: if we did that we would not have to worry about the bigger ones. So we made the crucial decision to limit our inquiries to a single day and that the most recent one: yesterday. We did not propose to ask the same people, day after day, what they had listened to the day before. We thought it wiser to question a different sample each day for if each day's sample was so selected as to be representative of the same population this would ensure that the findings for any day would be comparable with those of any other.

The limitation of our questions to a single day seemed to us to have practical psychological advantages. A day, rounded by sleep, is a natural unit of time in people's thinking. It should not be difficult to get people to recall yesterday, from rising to retiring, especially as, to aid accurate recall, we would exploit the principle of the association of ideas. So we would train our interviewers to start with some easily remembered event, usually but not necessarily getting up in the morning, and then to work onwards in time, reminding the informant of what had been on the radio and asking him/her whether or not he had heard it. (An interviewer who had not started her questioning with the beginning of the day would, having taken her informant up to bed-time, have to go back and cover the period before her starting point.)

But would people be willing to answer and, if they were,

would they answer truthfully? No one could be compelled to reply, so we would have to bear with some people refusing to co-operate. But there was already plenty of evidence from other social surveys suggesting that refusals would be comparatively rare, few enough for them not materially to affect the final picture. As to the truthfulness of answers, there were several problems to be contended with: the possibility that informants would say what they thought interviewers wanted them to say (or, maliciously, what they thought interviewers would *not* expect them to say); that they would say what would put them in the most favourable light (either in the interviewer's estimation or their own); and that, even given the best of intentions, they would make mistakes in recalling their listening.

To be sure we could not subpoena our sample to testify under oath, but there was a good deal we could do to maximise the likelihood that the truth would be told. Our approach was essentially positive: so to design the interview as at once to encourage accurate recall and discourage prevarication. The proper training of interviewers played an essential part in this. It was pointed out to them that they were at a psychological advantage when accosting strangers they hoped to interview; they held the initiative because they knew what they wanted while the 'subject' – some would say the 'victim' – did not. The subject would therefore tend to take his/her cue from the interviewer, so it was of the first importance that she should create the right frame of reference. This would depend not only on what she said (which we prescribed), but on the way she said it for in those first few seconds of the encounter the subject would, as it were, be 'listening to the music' as well as, if not more than, to the words.

We therefore made sure that interviewers knew exactly what the Survey of Listening was trying to do and the part its findings would play in the BBC's affairs. We impressed on them that their own role was crucial and that we wanted the facts about the public's listening regardless of whether these facts reflected credit on the BBC. A leaflet, which later grew into a *Handbook for Interviewers*, fore-armed them against difficulties they might encounter and they were assured that they could ring us up at any time for guidance. We tried to send them out confident and self-assured.

We also impressed on interviewers that speed was of the essence; helping an informant to recall a day need only take a few minutes once he/she understood what was wanted. This was embodied in the prescribed opening gambit: 'I am working for the BBC finding out what people listened to yesterday. Will you tell me what *you* listened to yesterday, please?' A pause at that point might be fatal, so the interviewer should pitch right in with some such question as: 'For instance, did you happen to switch on when you got up yesterday morning?' The informant might hesitate whereupon the interviewer might say: 'Well, what time was that, do you remember?' and having found out would say: 'That was when so-and-so was on. Did you hear that?' Before the informant had time to elaborate upon his answer he would be asked 'and what about (the next programme), did you listen to that?' or 'did you listen while you were having breakfast?'

This rapid approach was calculated to convey the impression to the informant that the interviewer was business-like and that the interview would not take long and also to encourage him to regard the encounter as a friendly challenge to him to see if he *could* remember something as recent as yesterday's listening. If he took it in this spirit, the focus of his attention might be diverted away from a possible preoccupation with the impression his replies were making on the interviewer. He would have told her all she wanted to know almost before he had realised he had done so. The deliberate prevaricator needs time, and time was just what he must not be given. Of course, once he had recounted his previous day's listening he might insist on elaborating on why it was not typical and how he always tried to hear x, y or z. In common courtesy the interviewer would have to make a written note of this, but no one would read it.

Some years later, when the BBC ceased to be a monopoly, we were criticised for continuing to instruct interviewers to open with the words 'I am working for the BBC ...' This, it was alleged, predisposed the informant to give replies which he thought the BBC would like to hear; in particular to exaggerate his BBC viewing and understate his viewing of ITV. This was certainly a plausible hypothesis, but it did not stand up to the test of experiment.

Two identical samples were questioned about their listening and viewing. The methods of questioning were also identical except that the interviews in one sample began with the conventional opening and those in the other had an introduction which omitted all reference to the BBC. When we compared the findings of the two samples we found they were virtually indistinguishable. So we did not revise our opening gambit, for interviewers liked being associated with the BBC and if it boosted their morale without distorting the findings we saw no reason to make a change.

We did not, of course, claim that the methods we used entirely eliminated prevarication or innocent error. Had we done so we would have had our come-uppance. The story is worth recounting. When the Survey started we did not ask interviewers to record the names or addresses of the people they interviewed: we took the view that this might increase the refusal rate. Later we decided that we must be in a position to check on whether interviews were really being made. For this we needed the names of informants so that we could subsequently write to a random selection of them and ask them to confirm that they had been interviewed. So we made the recording of names and addresses a requirement.

This did not in fact increase the refusal rate but it did have a disturbing result. The recorded quantity of listening to more serious programmes which, like all other programmes, had been astonishingly consistent, suddenly and sharply dropped to a lower, but equally consistent, level. Obviously something had been seriously wrong and that something could only be the quality of the interviewing force. Our system of recruiting and training was immediately overhauled.

From time to time after the war we laid on studies of the Survey's validity. We were primarily concerned about two possible sources of error; our use of the admittedly less-than-ideal quota method of sampling and our reliance on people's memory of the previous day. We therefore carried out studies, to run side by side with the Survey, in which the sample was selected by the Probability method and in which no demands at all were made on the informant's memory. Both these requirements could be fulfilled, though they were so costly as to be out of the question for normal daily working (for example, they involved restricting the yield of each interview to those programmes that were on the air at the moment when the interviewer rang the door-bell). Comparisons of the results of these criteria studies and the normal Survey were highly reassuring. They left us satisfied that the use of Quota sampling was fully justified and that our methods of Aided Recall, though capable of improvement, were basically sound.

When the Survey began, in December 1939, we had no interviewing force of our own so the fieldwork was carried out under contract by the British Institute of Public Opinion (later to be known as The Gallup Poll) whose Director was Henry Durant. Under this arrangement we specified what we wanted, designed the questionnaire and the interview and supplied BIPO with the forms (log-sheets) on which the results of the interviews were to be recorded. They hired (and sometimes fired) interviewers and delivered the completed logs to us for processing and the presentation of the results. But after it became clear that the Survey of Listening had come to stay the contract with BIPO was ended and in 1943 the Audience Research staff was enlarged to cope with the organisation of the fieldwork.

This involved us in recruiting and training a very large 'pool' of potential interviewers who could be called upon for spells of work when and where they were required. Interviewing for this Survey was always part-time work, taking about two to three hours a day, and it had to be intermittent if only because when on an 'assignment' the interviewer had to work a seven-day week. So the 'pool' had to be several times as large as the number of interviewers actually at work at any given moment.

Most of the interviewers were housewives, glad of the occasional pin-money. When I was appearing before the Parliamentary Labour Party's Committee on Broadcasting to explain what we did, its Chairman (Tony Greenwood) asked what qualities interviewing called for and what kinds of people we recruited. I said that we looked for conscientious, methodical people with a sense of responsibility, adding that really high-powered social investigators tended to find the simplicity of the interview rather beneath them. 'The people who make the best interviewers', I said, 'were the kind of people one found in WEA classes.' From the other side of the table came the gruff comment: 'Like us in fact.'

The daily sample had to be big enough to stand on its own feet, that is, to provide a reasonable degree of reliability for the estimates of the audiences of individual broadcasts, but no bigger, for that would have been wasteful. For as long as we only needed to present the findings in national terms we were content with 800 interviews each day, each of these daily samples being designed to represent the entire adult civilian population of Great Britain. (At first we did not cover Northern Ireland, nor children under the age of 16, but later the Survey was extended to include both.)

Some of my BBC colleagues were taken aback that I should recommend so small a sample as adequate to reflect the behaviour of a population of nearly 40 million. I tried to reassure them with the appropriate mathematical explanation but I have an uneasy feeling that their misgivings were set at rest less by this than by the fact that, day by day, the audience estimates which the Survey provided were so astonishingly consistent. In vain I would point out that consistency was no proof of validity; one could as easily be consistently wrong as consistently right.

The quota method by which we strove to ensure that the daily sample would be representative involved stipulating in advance, by relation to known statistics about the population, the number of interviews to be made in each BBC region and in urban and rural areas, to ensure proper geographical coverage, and also the number to be made with each sex, age group, the occupied and the unoccupied and each social class. The geographical quotas were achieved by appointing interviewers in designated places; the achievement of the other quotas was up to the interviewers. As an interviewer had only to cope with four age-groups (16–19, 20–29, 30–49 and 50 & over) she could usually 'place' most people on sight. We used three social classes: Upper Middle, Lower Middle, and Working Class. (I have never shared the squeamishness of some social research workers about the use of these terms which seem to me to be more vivid than artificial alphabetical labels.) The interviewer's problem in assigning an informant to one of these classes was made easier by the requirement that she should ask for the informant's occupation, for she was equipped with careful descriptions of the kinds of occupations we regarded as falling into each class. (Our criteria were more cultural than economic.)

We had frequently to stress that, as we were sampling the whole population and not merely the listening public, neither people who had not listened the previous day nor people who did not possess radio sets were *ipso facto* debarred from inclusion in the sample. Indeed if a day's sample failed to include due proportions of these groups it was to that extent unrepresentative of the population.

We were sometimes asked why we restricted the Survey of Listening to recording 'behaviour' – what people had listened to. 'Why', it was said, 'having located a listener to a programme, don't you take the opportunity to ask him what he thought of it?' (This had to be answered quite explicitly when, a couple of years later, we set up an entirely separate organisation to assess listeners' reactions to programmes.) There were several reasons. In the first place our Survey was not big enough for such a purpose. It was sufficient for measuring the sample's listening to a programme because every person questioned made a contribution to the answer; either positively (by saying he had listened to it) or negatively (by saying that he hadn't). But had we used the Survey to try to find out something about those who had listened to a programme, such as whether they had enjoyed it or not, only the answers of those who had listened to it would have been relevant and unless a very high proportion of the sample *had* listened to it their numbers would not have been sufficient to be a reliable basis for conclusions.

A second reason was that the kind of stream-lined interview we had designed for finding out what people had listened to was unsuitable as a vehicle for questions about audiences' reac-

Audience Research in War-time—I 97

tions (nor, for the matter of that, would all the interviewers we employed have been capable of asking them). Questions about attitudes and feelings usually call for thoughtful and considered answers; their inclusion would have demanded much longer interviews and have increased the cost of the whole operation far beyond what the BBC could have afforded.

And there was a third cogent reason. As it would have been quite impracticable to have asked questions about all programmes, we should have had to confine them to a selection. But this would have put paid to interviewers passing 'yesterday' smoothly and quickly under review; they would have had to pause at the programmes about which they had to ask supplementary questions. We were apprehensive about the consequences and with good reason for we tried it out and it had unfortunate results.

We did, however, frequently get interviewers to ask what we called Extra Questions (EQs) *after* they had completed the logging of the informant's listening. These EQs could relate to any issue of broadcasting concern – except the previous day's programmes. It was a facility which had to be restricted to matters which would admit of a limited number of pre-coded alternative answers, but it was useful whenever a count of heads was needed. A good example occurred in the summer of 1940 when the news was recording disaster after disaster. Both inside and outside the BBC there was an acute difference of opinion on whether this called for changes in the balance of output. The controversy about the broadcasting of light entertainment, which had died down during the phoney war, burst into fiercer flame. There were vehement assertions that this was wholly inappropriate at such a time; others were equally vehement that light and cheerful programmes kept peoples' spirits up and were never needed more.

So we posed this issue in the form of an EQ which read: 'When the news is grave do you think the BBC should cut down on variety programmes?' Over 60 per cent said 'No' and only about 20 per cent said 'Yes'. Analysis of the results showed that those who had said 'Yes' were in large part people who normally did not listen to variety programmes anyway. The conclusion we drew from this and other evidence was, as we said in our report at the time, '... tension has the effect, not of changing the normal tastes of the listening public, but of sharpening them'.

At about the same time an EQ was used to put another division of opinion into perspective: the perennial complaint about the broadcasting of what were then called Blue Jokes. That a number of listeners were distressed was evident from spontaneous correspondence, but how far were their protests representative of public opinion? We offered to try to find out and told our interviewers to ask all their informants to say which of these three statements came nearest to their own view:

> 'The BBC ought to be more careful in preventing its comedians from being vulgar.'
> 'The BBC is careful enough in preventing its comedians from being vulgar.'
> 'The BBC is too strict in preventing its comedians from being vulgar.'

The first of these statements was endorsed by 14 per cent, the second by 66 per cent and the third by 8 per cent (the remaining 12 per cent expressed no opinion). An analysis of these findings showed that the older the listener the more likely was he/she to feel the BBC ought to be more careful; that women endorsed this view more often than did men, and middle-class, more often than working-class, listeners. One listener supplemented his answer with the remark that 'BBC programmes are probably the cause of the amazing increase in crime and immortality [sic]'. Another, using an idiom which even thirty years ago seemed anachronistic, declared that BBC variety programmes 'debased the moral tone and standards of the lower classes'.

Interviewers were told not only how to begin their interviews but how to bring them to an end – a much-needed piece of guidance since some listeners saw this contact with a 'lady from the BBC' as a heaven-sent opportunity to unburden themselves. But even if the interviewee had all the time in the world the interviewer hadn't; her time was our money. As a long-stop she was instructed to say: '... and would you like me to put you down as satisfied or dissatisfied with current BBC programmes?' (Later we offered three alternative answers.)

Originally we had not expected the answers to this question to have any value in their own right but as time went on we realised that there were some lessons to be drawn from them. So we disseminated them as The BBC Thermometer because they threw light on the temperature of the public's feelings. At first the 'satisfied' clustered from day to day around 65 per cent and the 'dissatisfied' around 23 per cent (there were always a few 'don't knows'). Then, early in 1940, when a second radio service, the Forces Programme, was added to the Home Service, the 'satisfied' immediately jumped to 70 per cent and continued to increase until they levelled off at about 77 (with about 13 per cent 'dissatisfied'). Although in the years that followed the 'satisfied' were always the great majority, there were some puzzling minor fluctuations. Then it occurred to me to relate the Thermometer to the news of the day. At once the mists lifted. When the news was bad, as it frequently was, the proportion of the population who were dissatisfied with the BBC invariably rose – an echo perhaps of the monarchical practice of executing the man who brought the bad news.

This pattern continued until the war in Europe ended; then, quite suddenly, it stopped; for several years the BBC Thermometer hardly fluctuated at all from day to day. But one day in 1949 there was a sharp drop in the number of people who said they were dissatisfied with the BBC. It was the day when the news was announced of the sudden death of Tommy Handley, the central character of *Itma*, the most successful and best-loved of the war-time light entertainment shows. No one who was around at the time will need to be reminded of the astonishing impact of this news. It was a day of spontaneous national mourning. We could only conclude that when people were asked that day whether they were satisfied or dissatisfied with BBC programmes, many of the normally disgruntled 'didn't feel they could criticise the BBC On A Day Like This.'

The results these EQs yielded were no more than useful by-products. The primary purpose, indeed the *raison d'etre*, of the Survey was the production of a daily 'barometer' giving estimates of the magnitude of the audiences of all the programmes which had been broadcast in the domestic services. A programme's 'listening figure', as it was often called, was in fact the percentage of the sample interviewed which had been recorded as having listened to it – but by inference it was the approximate proportion of the adult civilian population in the audience.

But how approximate was 'approximate'? Precise statements of the sampling error could, strictly speaking, only be made had the sample been selected by the Probability method (explained in Chapter 3). Ours, for reasons of practicality, were chosen by the Quota method. But there was good reason to believe that if Quota sampling were carried out well its sampling error would not be very different. If so then, with a daily sample of 800 as ours at first was, the odds were 19:1 that a listening figure of 40 per cent would represent an audience somewhere between $36\frac{1}{2}$ per cent and $43\frac{1}{2}$ per cent of the population surveyed; that a figure of 20 per cent would indicate an audience somewhere between 17 per cent and 23 per cent and one of 10 per cent an audience of between 8 per cent and 12 per cent.

Most broadcasts were, of course, either in series or, like *News Bulletins*, at fixed times each day. In such cases interest centred on the trend of their audiences. We often had to discourage people from taking too much notice of small fluctuations, pointing out that, in the nature of sampling, modest variations of no statistical significance were to be expected – as, indeed, were very occasional freak figures. We tried to encourage people to place greater reliance on averages over time than on individual figures – the more cases an average was based on, the greater the reliability. Thus an average of ten cases would be based on the evidence culled from 8,000 interviews.

The Listening Barometer was often referred to as the BBC's Box Office. Naturally producers were primarily interested in its findings about the broadcasts for which they were responsible. Programme planners on the other hand were equally, if not more, interested in what they could learn about the levels of listening at different times of day, on different days of the week at different seasons, in different regions and to different services. Quite soon, therefore, we developed a series of tables which were brought up to date, and circulated, weekly so that trends could be kept under constant review.

There were always those who wanted audience estimates expressed as numbers of people instead of as percentages of population. I never encouraged this, though I had to do it myself in articles for popular consumption. I disliked it for several reasons. It seemed to me, illogically perhaps, to lend a spurious air of precision to what professed to be no more than approximations. It was clumsy, too, since when expressed in numbers most audiences ran to seven digits. But there was a deeper reason: it seemed to me that the currency given to statements that this or that programme 'had an audience of so many million people' inevitably implied that there was some special virtue in mere bigness. To be sure the converse – that virtue lay in smallness – was no less indefensible, but it was, perhaps, less dangerous because its overtones of arrogance would be so obvious.

I called the assertion that 'Bigger invariably meant Better' the Quantitative Fallacy. It is a vulgar error because it is either tautological or without meaning. If the criterion of programme quality is simply the size of the audience then the assertion is tautological. But if there is some other, unspecified, criterion the statement is meaningless. But perhaps the distaste I felt at expressing audiences in numbers really reflected my difficulty in living with the knowledge that in providing the BBC with a box office I was inevitably making it easier for people to fall into the Quantitative Fallacy.

Two final points: we were sometimes chided for attaching so much importance to knowing what people *had* listened to. What about the programmes they *would have* listened to, if only they had been broadcast? A good question, but an extremely difficult one to investigate. How could programmes of kinds which people had never yet heard be effectively described? Would anyone have thought *The Goon Show* attractive if all they knew about it was a written specification? It takes a lively imagination to conjure up the taste of a new dish from reading the recipe.

It was also argued that as people were frequently prevented

from listening to what they were interested in, their actual listening was no reflection of their preferences. The only reply to that was the last year's performance is a notoriously better guide to next year's behaviour than are New Year resolutions.

7 Audience Research in War-time—II

At the same time as we were launching the continuous Survey of Listening we began to set up our network of Honorary Local Correspondents (HLCs). Its function, as was said in the last chapter, was to act as a means for keeping the BBC in touch with public opinion in so far as this was relevant to broadcasting. There was no way in which we could ensure that, taken together, the reports the HLCs sent us were a demonstrably valid sample of the population. It would therefore be out of the question to quantify them; we would have to 'take the sense of the meeting' rather than count heads. Usually this presented little difficulty; a broad and unmistakable consensus would emerge, divergent views being manifestly those of minorities. When there was no obvious consensus we would simply spell out the diverging views without attempting to assess their relative strength.

Eventually we appointed over 2,000 HLCs and made it a practice to send them monthly questionnaires which usually covered several issues. The corps was divided into four comparable sub-sections to which different questionnaires could be sent if necessary. This quadrupled its capacity without increasing the burden on individual Correspondents. The issues put to them were many and various. For example, in the summer of 1940 they were asked what people felt about Charles Gardiner's much discussed Running Commentary on an aerial dog-fight over the cliffs of Dover; the following December they were asked whether or not there was a demand for more talks about the war effort; in 1941 views were sought, *inter-alia*, on whether eye-witness accounts, dispatches etc. included in news bulletins, should be segregated from the factual news; on the distribution of time between different types of output and on the demand for 'recorded repeats' of variety shows.

A body of Forces Correspondents was enrolled to reflect the views of the primary target for the Forces Programme, which had begun early in 1940. Though its sights were set on the B.E.F. and the Forces at home, it was also in effect a second channel for the civilian population and soon became the preferred channel for most of them. For the most part the content of the Forces Programme consisted of traditional light entertainment (indeed its grandchild, after the war, was the BBC Light Programme), but it was in no small measure as a direct result of evidence collected from our Forces Correspondents that a regular magazine programme of 'something to think about' was introduced into the Forces Programme. This was *Ack-Ack Beer-Beer*, designed to meet the special needs of men and women serving on often remote anti-aircraft sites where life consisted of long hours of boredom punctuated by short periods of all too exciting activity.

Ironically the sire of this programme, which was a resounding success, was a pacifist, Roger Wilson. Before the war, Roger, a Quaker, had been an outstandingly bright talks producer in Manchester. But a timorous BBC did not feel that a professed pacifist should be a producer of talks in war-time. I asked if he could come to help me and this was agreed. I asked him to set up the network of Forces Correspondents which he did with conspicuous and characteristic efficiency. Later that year the BBC 'released' Roger from BBC service for the duration. At just about the same time my Deputy, Bobby Cockburn, volunteered for military service so we held a joint farewell party to which the incongruity added a piquancy.

To replace them I took on two men from outside the BBC: F. H. Littman and Eric Mosley. Fred Littman was already a close personal friend. He had been in publishing until the war left him high and dry. I knew him to have the right cast of mind so I asked him if he would like to join me. I had no difficulty in persuading my then Controller, Nicholls, that Fred was the right man when he found that they had frequently had a midday swim together at the Marshall Street Baths. Fred soon became Assistant Head of Listener Research, a post he held until his retirement in 1963, after which he edited for us an enormous reference book, *The People's Activities*, and then went to Dublin to start up audience research for Radio Eireann. Fred was the ideal choice; a quiet, omnicompetent, unflappable man who got through a prodigious amount of work without fuss. His judgements were shrewd and he inspired both confidence and affection, particularly amongst our growing junior staff. In more than twenty-five years' working association I do not recall a single instance of friction between us but I do recall countless occasions when I was in his debt.

My other senior recruit, Eric Mosley came from the world of adult education. At 14 he had gone to work in the pits but had subsequently won a trade union scholarship to Oxford from which he had moved into academic life. A dark, stocky man with an irresistible and disarming grin and an insatiable appetite for work, Eric was totally without affectation. It was he who built up our 'audience reaction' side. We enjoyed him for several years but he left after the war to become Welfare Officer for the newly formed National Dock Labour Board. Later he became a Senior Labour Relations Officer for the N.C.B. in the East Midlands. Both he and Fred Littman married members of my staff.

A notable combined operation in which both the HLCs and the Survey of Listening were involved took place soon after they were both set up. It was a study called *Hamburg Broadcast Propaganda*. In the last few years before the outbreak of war the use of broadcasting to influence foreign opinion had become very common. The Italian and the German broadcasting organisations had set the pace and, with some distaste, the BBC had fallen into step. When the war began the British public became increasingly aware of German broadcasts in English from Hamburg and of the voice of its principal reader, William Joyce (Lord Haw Haw). No inquiry was necessary to establish that he had a considerable audience in this country for his broadcasts began to be a common topic of conversation, but no one knew with any precision what kind of people were listening, what credence they were giving to what he said and what effect his broadcasts were having.

The Ministry of Information asked the BBC to get its Audience Research Department to study the problem and we jumped at the opportunity. The work was done in the winter of 1939/40. Three forms of inquiry were used. The Continuous Survey of Listening played its part; using the EQ technique described in the last chapter, data was collected about the nightly extent of listening to Hamburg. The HLCs gathered information about what people were saying about the Hamburg broadcasts. The third form of inquiry was novel. Knowing that it would be useless to ask listeners to Hamburg to say whether or not they were influenced by its broadcasts (they either wouldn't know or wouldn't tell), we commissioned a special public opinion survey, with a sample of 5,000. Some of the questions related to issues which Hamburg was constantly plugging and others to issues which Hamburg ignored. At the same time the informants were asked how often they listened to the news (from the BBC and from Hamburg) and what papers they read.

The inquiry confirmed that listening to Hamburg was widespread. Each night in early December 1939 about one person in four would listen to the news from Hamburg; about two-thirds of the population could be said to be occasional, if not regular, listeners to it. Men listened more often than did women and the younger half of the population more than the older half. Listening also increased with each step up the social scale. But these were not the only ways in which listening was analysed. It was also related to newspaper-reading and to listening to BBC news. These comparisons were particularly revealing for listening to Hamburg was quite evidently not a substitute for, but a supplement to, listening to the BBC; those who listened most to BBC news were also those who listened most to Hamburg. In terms of newspaper-reading, the heaviest Hamburg listeners were readers of *The Times* and the quality press and the lightest were the readers of the two tabloids, the *Daily Sketch* and the *Daily Mirror*. Hamburg's broadcast propaganda was often specifically directed to those whose bread-winners or sons had joined the forces or who had already suffered hardship because of the war, but our inquiry found that these groups listened to Hamburg no more and no less than the rest of the population.

The evidence from the HLCs showed that most commonly professed motives for listening to Haw Haw because 'his version of the news was so fantastic that it is funny,' because 'so many other people listen to him and talk about it' and because people were 'amused at his voice and manner'. To a lesser extent the admitted motives were to 'hear the German point of view' and to 'get more news'. As the summary of the final report said 'the blackout, the novelty of hearing the enemy, the desire to hear both sides, the insatiable appetite for news and the desire to be in the swim have all played their part in the build-up of Hamburg's audience and in holding it together. The entertainment value of the broadcasts; their concentration of undeniable evils in this country; their news sense; their presentation; the publicity they have received in this country, together with the momentum of the habit of listening to them, have all contributed towards their esablishment as a familiar feature of the social landscapes.' There was little or no evidence from this source that listening to Hamburg reflected distrust with news from British sources, still less sympathy with the Nazi point of view, though, to be sure, had people felt this way they would, in the prevailing climate of opinion, have been unlikely to admit it.

The public opinion survey, as has been said, was designed to reveal any correlations which might exist between listening to Haw Haw and attitudes towards some of the specific issues which had been the recurrent theme of his broadcasts. We chose five of them: the disunity of the British Empire; the achievements of Nazi rule in raising the living standards of the German people; the unfairness of the British rationing system; the allegations that the British Government was concealing the full extent of British naval losses and that the chief beneficiaries of the war would certainly *not* be 'Britain and France' or 'the working classes'. Each was cast in question form, the last, for example, read; 'Do you think any of the following are likely to gain out of the war: Soviet Russia, the Nazis, big business, America, the Jews, the working classes, Britain and France, none of these?'

In some cases the replies of regular Hamburg listeners did come nearer than those of non-listeners to the pattern which the German Propaganda Ministry obviously wanted. For example, the regular Hamburg listeners were better informed about which parts of the Empire were 'not fully with us', were more suspicious that our naval losses were not being fully disclosed (and less inclined to accept this policy) and were more disposed to believe that Hitler had, before the war, 'raised the living standards of ordinary people in Germany' and that it would be America and big business which would be likely to gain most out of the war. But the attitudes of regular Hamburg listeners were no different from those of non-listeners towards the British rationing.

An important point which had to be taken into account when considering the evidence of this inquiry was that anyone who took any interest in public affairs would recognise that Hamburg's line on these issues was quite subtle. They were not so much trying to disseminate downright falsehoods as to exploit undeniable facts in such a way as to excite 'alarm and despondency'. With Eire neutral, South Africa deeply divided and India concerned above all with achieving freedom, the disunity of 'the Empire' as compared with its unity in 1914 was undeniable; the Nazi Government had indeed reduced unemployment in Germany, if only by its rearmament programme; the British rationing system was not perfect (but what rationing system ever was?). As long as America remained neutral she might well benefit from the war. It went without saying in Britain that Germany would lose the war, so 'the Jews', as many of the sample pointed out, would certainly benefit – by the end of their persecution. Perhaps we were not being told the full extent of our Naval losses, but if concealment was intended to confuse the enemy it was justified.

It followed from this that people whose answers to our questions accorded with what Hamburg was saying had not necessarily been persuaded by it – they might quite well be expressing views which they would have held anyway. Had this evidence stood alone the verdict would have been not proven. But it did not. There were the answers to the other questions – those related to issues Hamburg was not plugging; the evi-

Audience Research in War-time—II 109

dence about Hamburg listeners' newspaper reading and BBC news listening habits; evidence that the regular Hamburg listeners tended as a group to be better informed, more alert and generally more interested in public affairs than non-listeners (invariably far more of the non-listeners than of the regular Hamburg listeners expressed no opinion). These considerations led us to the conclusion that listening to Hamburg was having little effect in influencing public opinion.

The final report did, however, contain a warning. It was speculative but not, I think, unjustified and read: 'This study has been made in the context of a relatively static war. It is safe to say that, as yet, widespread hatred of the enemy does not exist. But if there were widespread suffering, hatred might grow and the task of the Hamburg propagandist would become correspondingly difficult. If there was widespread social discontent, on the other hand, this would be Hamburg's opportunity. It is certain that the impact of Hamburg's propaganda should be kept under constant observation.'

We did keep it under constant observation in the years that followed and what happened was instructive. As soon as the phoney war ended with the German invasion of Scandinavia, followed soon after by the invasion of Holland and Belgium, the collapse of France and the evacuation from Dunkirk, Hamburg's nightly British audiences began to shrink. Ultimately they dwindled to relatively insignificant dimensions and so remained for the rest of the war. It was as though the British people had decided that it was time to put away the childish things.

For the Audience Research Department itself the London blitz brought an upheaval. In mid-September in common with other departments; we were moved out of London. We left it with mixed feelings. For myself, though I am no hero and quaked during the nightly bombings as much as the next man, I was conscious of a pang of regret at being sent out of the front line (though as it turned out we had our fair share of bombing in Bristol to which we were sent). We set up shop in an empty house in Clifton and resumed normal activities as quickly as we could. The Continuous Survey of Listening had to be suspended for a week while we moved – the only break in its continuity for more than thirty years. Soon after we got there we finally lost Roger Wilson (he was soon organising Friends War Relief) but we kept the rest of our staff who were billeted round about.

To return to the use we made of the HLCs: *pace* the cliché, they enabled us to keep the BBC's finger on the public's pulse. And that is where it needed to be, especially in war-time, with the public dependent on radio as never before. Although most of the questions we asked were directly related to programmes and the business of broadcasting, sometimes this link was more remote. For example, when the USA entered the war the British public's interest in, and need for, information about it took a new turn and presented new challenges to the BBC. In preparation we put the HLCs on to the job of assessing current attitudes towards America. The findings of inquiries such as these would sometimes do no more than confirm suppositions – and there was value in that – but they would sometimes throw up unexpected leads. When, in the last year of the war, the BBC embarked on large-scale forward-looking series of talks on such subjects as Housing and Employment after the war (*Homes for All* and *Jobs for All*) the HLCs played a similar role.

In practice it was largely left to us to decide what the HLC should be asked to report upon: we conceived it to be our job to sense needs before they became clamant. If we had waited to be asked to launch inquiries the request would often have come too late for us to be able to satisfy it effectively. The exercise of this discretion was to land me in my only unpleasant encounter with a Director-General. When it became obvious that the end of the war was approaching the press began discussing the shape of peace-time Britain including, naturally, the future of broadcasting. I thought it would be of value to the Corporation to know what ordinary people thought about this so I sent a questionnaire to HLCs asking, among other things, how they thought people would react to sponsored radio. They had already plenty of opportunity to know what it was like because most of them had heard Radios Luxembourg and Normandie before the war.

We did not publicise the questionnaire but the fact that we

had sent it out appeared in the press and I was summoned by Haley, then Director-General. When I entered his room I could see that there was trouble. His expression made me appreciate J. B. Priestley's remark that Haley was the only man he had ever met who had two glass eyes.

Haley first asked me if the press reports were true. I said that substantially they were and explained my reasons for launching the inquiry. He said that he accepted my explanation but regarded it as the worst error of judgement he had come across since he came to the BBC. The questionnaire must be publicly withdrawn and no similar inquiries must be launched without his consent – which was fair enough, though in fact none was subsequently vetoed. With that the interview ended. What I did not know then – I only heard it years afterwards – was that the question of the post-war shape of broadcasting was already under discussion at Ministry level so that my action had unwittingly caused Haley considerable embarrassment. In the circumstances his anger was fully justified. I was still smarting under his rebuke, when later that night, I found myself standing next to Haley in a place where men do stand briefly side by side. Impulsively I turned to him and said that what worried me most after our conversation that morning was that I might now have forfeited his confidence altogether. His reply was characteristic: 'If I had meant that, that is what I should have said. Now forget it.'

I did forget it in the sense that it did not colour my future dealings with him. He was tough but he was just, as was shown by another incident which occurred just after D-Day – the day of the Normandy invasion. The BBC had made elaborate arrangements to follow the *Nine o'clock News* with the first edition of *War Report* which would bring listeners the recorded voices of its war correspondents who had landed on the beaches with the troops that morning. Such an enterprise was at that time quite new and Haley rightly set great store by it. But when the Listening Barometer for that day arrived on his table he found to his chagrin that we had no audience estimate for the first *War Report*. He wrote me a reproachful note pointing out that this was perhaps the most important broadcast the BBC had ever put out and our failure to measure its audience was lamentable.

I replied that I agreed but that there were good reasons. To have arrived at an estimate of *War Report*'s audience would have necessitated printing it, as a numbered item, on the Log Sheets sent to interviewers in advance. But the precise day on which the invasion would take place was top secret. Had we been party to the secret it would obviously have been wildly irresponsible to include it in papers that were printed some days before. But of course, we were not. I told him that we had considered printing it as the next item after the *Nine o'clock News* every day around the period when everyone expected the invasion to take place, telling interviewers to ignore it if it did not turn out to be applicable, but we decided against this on the grounds that this might have started rumours and done damage. Haley replied that he was fully satisfied with my explanation. 'The important thing is' he said 'that the question had been thought about.'

In fact Haley took a more active and intelligent interest in audience research than most of the other Directors-General under whom I served. My professional dealings with him after the war will be referred to in a later chapter but I am anticipating one incident because it throws a light on Haley as a man. In the Autumn of 1947 I received an offer of a post outside the BBC which was not only attractive and challenging as a job but would also have meant a considerable increase in my earnings. I at once wrote to tell Haley of this, saying that I had not made up my mind, that I was happy in the BBC and would leave it with great reluctance, but that the salary offered was tempting as I had three children to educate. He thanked me for telling him of the offer, said he would be sorry if I left and that if I stayed my salary would be increased – though not, as I knew it could not be in view of the BBC's then salary policy, by enough to match the offer I had had. But he added that he would not blame me if, even so, I decided to accept it.

After further thought I did accept it and resigned from the BBC. My contract stipulated three months' notice but before a few weeks had passed I began to have trouble with my sight. (Of course it occurred to me that this might be a case of cause and effect but this thought, though interesting, was not particularly helpful.) The condition, which worsened until I was virtually blind, stubbornly resisted treatment. When I asked for a prognosis I was told that the recovery of my sight was problematical. The doctors were much more pessimistic to my wife who was keeping the BBC informed. When she reported this Haley wrote: 'Tell your husband that if he wishes to withdraw his resignation he is welcome to do so.' Needless to say I gratefully accepted this offer. In fact I recovered my sight and returned to duty after a six months' absence to find that Haley had given instructions that my salary should be increased to the figure he had said it would be had I not resigned.

During the second War winter, 1940–1, I came to feel more and more that in a properly balanced audience research service the continuous measurement of the quantity of listening – the estimation of the size of each programme's audience – should be supplemented by a continuous assessment of audience reaction – what listeners' felt about the programmes they were listening to. So long as quantitative data alone was pouring out from Audience Research day after day there was a real danger that the bigger-necessarily-means-better heresy would gain adherents by default. Besides, however useful as a substitute for the box office, there were functions quantitative data could not fulfil. Knowing the size of a programme's audience told one nothing about the nature of that audience's listening experience, what it was about the programme that they had liked or not liked or why they felt about it as they did.

Moreover, from an examination of the pattern of the public's listening it soon became apparent that the size of a programme's audience was the product of many causes of which the programme itself was only one. Without any change in the content of a programme, the size of its audience could be radically altered simply by transmitting it at a different time or by changing its placing; put it immediately after, or even immediately before, a programme which had a large following and its audience went up. Even a mere change of title could make a difference. No series of Chamber Music programmes ever attracted a substantial following until someone thought of leaving those fatal words out of the billing and calling it simply *Music in Miniature*.

Of course if box-office takings and the applause of the audience were simply different indicators of the same thing – in other words if the size of a broadcasts' audience were predictive of that audience's reactions on hearing it, or vice versa – then there would be no point in measuring both. But it was inconceivable that this could be so. Everyone knew there could be cases of small theatre audiences being delighted with what they saw and large audiences being indifferent or downright disappointed, and the same must be true of broadcasting.

Our pre-war experiments in using panels to reflect audience reactions had shown that we had a method to hand so I put the case to Nicholls, as Controller of Programmes, and found him sympathetic. I suggested that we should fill the gap by setting up listening panels on a permanent basis, appeal for volunteers to man them and with their aid undertake to produce, in the first instance, reports on the audiences' reactions to about fifteen different programmes a week. (This would, of course, be only a fragment of the output but it would be enough to enable us to play the searchlight over programmes and so keep the output in general under pretty constant review.)

The plan was agreed to and the operation got under way in 1941. We set up a Music Panel, a Plays Panel and a Women's Panel (mainly for daytime programmes) and also two General Listening Panels to cope with other kinds of output. (Later the last three were replaced by a Features Panel, a Talks and Discussion Panel and a Light Entertainment Panel.) Each had 500 members. In a talk on the air and in a *Radio Times* article, supplemented by a press handout, I explained the scheme and invited listeners to volunteer to help. Within a very short time about 10,000 had done so (they were referred to in a *Times* Third Leader as 'The Noble Ten Thousand').

Each volunteer was sent a Detail Form asking for further information about himself and his tastes so that we could assign people to the panel where they would be most useful and at the same time make its composition correspond as nearly as we could to that of the particular public which it was to represent. We were under no illusions about this method of recruiting. It would not produce the same kind of panel as would have been obtained had we been able to call upon random samples of each public. We knew it opened the door to volunteer-bias (already discussed in Chapter 4) but we went ahead in the faith, based on previous experience, that though what we should learn of audiences' reaction from these panels might be an exaggerated version of the facts, it would not be a seriously distorted version. Perhaps a simpler way to put it would be that we should be learning about the reactions of the keener listeners rather than of listeners generally.

Those whose services we could not use immediately were placed in a reserve on which we drew when replacements were required. Each week the panel member was sent questionnaires relating to between three and six forthcoming broadcasts of their own speciality. They were not required to listen to those broadcasts, indeed we urged them not to vary from normal listening habits on our account but merely to complete the appropriate questionnaire if they happened to hear the broadcast to which it related. As a result the number of questionnaires returned varied from broadcast to broadcast, those with big audiences yielding the biggest and those with small the smallest, number of completed questionnaires. As in the various pre-war panels, the questionnaires were tailor-made for each broadcast; they were quite brief, normally having four or five questions. These questions were designed to elicit listeners' feelings about different aspects of the broadcast – the acting, the production and the script of plays; the subject of a discussion and the contribution of the different participants; the various acts in a vaudeville; the vividness of a running commentary and the intrinsic interest of the event being broadcast and so on.

One question was common to all questionnaires: this was a request to the panel member to award marks to the programme 'out of ten'. More precisely, the panel member was asked to use this opportunity to indicate the degree of enjoyment he had derived from listening (though it wasn't put in precisely these words). He was only to award ten if he enjoyed the broadcast so much that he could not imagine enjoying it more, and zero only if he detested it. It was listeners' subjective feelings we were trying to measure, not their objective assessments of the programme's merits. (Most panel members found this distinction incomprehensible – the programmes they liked were 'good' and those they disliked were *ipso facto* 'bad'.)

From the marks awarded we calculated what we called an Appreciation Index. This was simply the average mark multiplied by ten. Appreciation Indexes were intended to facilitate comparisons between the extent to which broadcasts (of similar genre) had been enjoyed. It is hardly necessary to stress that we discouraged comparisons of broadcasts of dissimilar types like church services and boxing commentaries.

Being in effect the degree of enjoyment of the average listener, the Appreciation Index had one obvious potential disadvantage: the 'average listener' was an abstraction and though in most cases there would be many like him, there would be some cases where he corresponded to none. This could happen if the audience's reactions were sharply polarised; if one half were ecstatic and the other half bored to distraction, the arithmetic average of the marks awarded would describe none of them. We kept a sharp watch for such cases but in fact they were very rare; the curves of the distribution of marks seldom had two humps (or, as the statistician would say, were seldom bi-modal).

What we did find, however, was that the marks awarded tended to cluster in the top half of the 0–10 scale (perhaps because, remembering their school-days, people tended to 'start off' with ten and then knock off marks for things they didn't like). This was unfortunate for it meant that most Appreciation Indexes lay between sixty-five and eighty-five, making it often difficult to decide whether a difference of one or two points was significant or merely the result of chance, For this reason, when the system was revamped after the war, we abandoned the marks-out-of-ten basis and went over to a five-point alphabetical scale, A+, A, B, C, and C− with verbal equivalents set out thus:

A + stands for
- 'I wouldn't have missed this programme for anything'
- *or* 'I can't remember when I enjoyed (liked) a programme so much'
- *or* 'One of the most interesting (amusing, moving, impressive) programmes I have ever heard'

A stands for
- 'I am very glad indeed that I didn't miss this'
- or 'I enjoyed (liked) it very much indeed'
- or 'Very interesting (amusing, moving, impressive) indeed'

B stands for
- 'I found this quite a pleasant (satisfactory) programme'
- or 'I quite enjoyed (liked) it'
- or 'A quite interesting (amusing) programme'
- or 'A rather moving (impressive) programme'

C stands for
- 'I felt listening to this was rather a waste of time'
- or 'I didn't care for this much'
- or 'It was rather dull (boring, feeble)'

C − stands for
- 'I felt listening to this was a complete waste of time'
- or 'I disliked it very much'
- or 'It was very dull (boring, feeble)'

It will be apparent that these statements aimed to establish the middle point, B, as normality and to try to get Panel members to keep the extremes, A+ and C−, in reserve for really exceptionally enjoyable (or repellant) broadcasts.

For presentation purposes we still expressed Appreciation Indexes 'out of 100' by awarding points to each position on the scale (from four down to zero); the Index being the number of points scored as a percentage of the maximum possible. This new system certainly reduced the general run of Indexes, though not by as much as we had hoped. They now clustered around sixty to sixty-five and with that we had to be content.

Perhaps the most important role fulfilled by disseminating Appreciation Indices alongside estimates of audience size was to bring home the fact that the pleasure/pain a broadcast had given could not be judged from the size of its audience. Appreciation Indices and audience sizes moved quite independently; often when two broadcasts of a similar kind were compared one would be found to have the larger audience but the other the higher Appreciation Index.

The replies to each questionnaire were written up in a report which went to the people most concerned – the producer, the head of his department and the planners (though it was available for anyone in the BBC to see). The report would show the size of the broadcast's audience (as estimated by the Survey of Listening) and its Appreciation Index, both with appropriate comparisons, followed by the digest of the answers to the various questions.

Although these reports conformed to a standard pattern we did our best to make them readable, where possible quoting the actual words of panel members to illustrate points of view. Sometimes a comment had to be included in its own right, as when a panel member who had heard the Dorothy Sayers' cycle of plays *A Man Born to be King* in which Robert Speight played the part of Jesus wrote '... and I was particularly delighted to find the part of Christ played by an old Haileyburian.'

A reaction report did not purport to be more than a picture of how a broadcast had been received by its audience – insofar as panel members who had sent in completed questionnaires represented them. It made no claim to be a critical evaluation in any professional sense. Since listeners did not divest themselves of their predilections or prejudices before they listened at home, we didn't ask panel members to do so before they answered our questions. If they did not understand what the producer or writer was getting at, blamed him for failing to do something he wasn't trying to do, or reacted in other ways which he thought irrelevant, their reactions might irritate or exasperate him but it was as well for him to know that that was how his broadcast had been received.

It would have been impossible for us to have produced reaction reports on every broadcast, nor was it necessary that we should do so, but from the first we covered a substantial proportion of them – to begin with about five hundred a year which increased after the war to about three thousand. The choice was a matter for negotiation. Producers would ask for reports and so could heads of output departments. The final choice was made in consultation with the service editors, a consultation in which Audience Research frequently took the initiative.

This complement to audience measurement soon caught on and proved of value in a number of different ways. In general it served to encourage those whose job it was to produce broadcasts which, by their very nature, could not hope to attract the big battalions but which nevertheless could mean a great deal to their listeners. And even in the arena where the big boys contended it was often salutary to be able to show that, for listeners, bigger did not always betoken better.

We were often told that the findings of our reaction reports were predictable; indeed they often were, but the predictions of a producer, the head of his department and the editor of the service which had commissioned the broadcast were not always identical – to put it mildly. In such cases the findings of audience research came into their own as outside and independent confirmation of one of the conflicting predictions.

We were pleased when word reached us of a comment by Norman Corwin, a distinguished American guest producer, when he was shown a reaction report on the BBC production of one of his plays, 'Gosh this is marvellous, we have nothing like this in our country.'

8 From War to Peace

We had been brought back from the West Country in the summer of 1942. We were housed in a block of luxury flats in Portland Place next to the Chinese Embassy. In its basement Dr Sun Yat-Sen had once been incarcerated until he attracted the attention of a passing policeman by thrusting a note through the grating at ground level. There we spent the rest of the war, emerging unscathed from the V1s, which fell uncomfortably close, and the V2s, which fell without warning.

One big advantage of our new premises was their nearness to Regent's Park. Soon after bombardment began in June 1944 I slipped in, as usual, at lunchtime to find that in the night a flying-bomb had fallen and left a huge crater. The park around it seemed just as it had been except for one tree – an enormous beech – a few feet from where the bomb had fallen. It still stood firmly rooted, but it was stripped of every vestige of foliage. The sight was obscene. I could not bring myself to pass that spot for a week or two, but when I did I was humbled; from every branch there was a fresh growth of tiny leaf.

A year later, in May 1945, the war in Europe was over. Those who have grown up in the television age can have little appreciation of the place of radio in everyday existence in Britain during the war. It was above all the main source of news. The news bulletins invariably stood out as peaks in the daily listening curve: the largest were at six and nine p.m. when on a typical day their audiences would be anything from 30 to 50 per cent of the population. On special occasions, as when it was known that the Prime Minister would speak, listening audiences would be even greater—usually over 60 per cent. On the evening of D-Day, by which time it was known

From War to Peace 121

that the Allied Armies had at last landed in Normandy, 80 per cent listened at nine p.m.

We all knew, of course, that the enormous appetite for news was a direct result of the war and we all expected it to slacken off once peace came. What we didn't expect was the immediate and spectacular fall in news bulletin listening that occurred as soon as hostilities in Europe ended. It was as though the curtain had rung down and the audience – or half of them – had promptly left the hall. From then on it was never possible again to count on audiences of 60 to 70 per cent for anything except royal weddings and the broadcasts from Sandringham on Christmas Day.

In other respects the pattern of the public's taste, as reflected by the broadcasts they chose to hear, did not change when the war was over. (They probably had not changed when the war began but we had no adequate basis for comparison.) Once their need for news was satisfied, people looked to broadcasting then, as they do now, for entertainment and relaxation; though as to what constituted entertainment and relaxation there were, and always will be, many differing opinions.

Anyone who studied the Listening Barometer carefully from day to day soon became aware that, within fairly broad limits, the size of the audiences for individual broadcasts was predictable. There were, of course, variations attributable to such factors as time of day, the service which happened to be transmitting the broadcast or the accidents of placing but, these aside, the limits within which audiences varied in size depended on the type of programme to which they belonged. Those for light entertainment shows in mid-evening, for example, would lie between 20 and 45 per cent of the population, plays and features between about 15 and 30 per cent and symphony concerts between about 5 and 10 per cent.

It became clear that, even in the most propitious circumstances, it was most unlikely that any broadcast would achieve an audience falling outside the limits for its type. Its potential audience was thus not the whole of the population but a segment of it which consisted of the 'following', or the 'public', for that type of material. As we had found in our attempts to identify the tastes of the population (described in Chapter 4), it wasn't easy to draw a hard and fast line between those who were, and those who were not, to be considered as members of a 'public'. While there would be no difficulty about placing either devotees or those to whom the type was anathema, it would be difficult to decide on where the cutting-point should be in that part of the spectrum where tepid interest shaded into indifference. But this did not invalidate the concept: each type of programme had its own public and it was from amongst them that the vast majority of the audiences of broadcasts of that type would be drawn. The population was thus not monolithic; it consisted of a number of different publics, of widely differing sizes and certainly not mutually exclusive for any listener might be a 'member' of many.

But what explained the differences between the magnitudes of the various publics? Why was that for light entertainment so large and that for Chamber Music so small? Why did so many more people like plays than like Opera? The one hypothesis which seemed to fit all the facts had to do with the extent to which the enjoyment of a type of broadcasting made demands upon the listener; the greater the demands, the smaller the public.

The demands made by broadcasts could be of varying kinds. Some broadcasts would be meaningless if they were not followed closely, in the very nature of things they demand undivided attention. Some broadcasts could not really be enjoyed unless the listener had some previous knowledge, for instance, at least some knowledge of the rules of cricket is a pre-requisite for enjoying a commentary from Lords. Listening to a broadcast may make demands on the listener's powers of imagination, capacity for empathy or just plain curiosity; it may demand that he suspend – or at least re-arrange – his prejudices.

It is not, of course, particularly surprising that the more demanding a broadcast, the fewer the people who will want to listen to it. For most people, most of the time, listening – and viewing television – must be seen as forms of play which are indulged in at home, for 'free'. Listening to the radio is play in the sense that it is undertaken for its own sake and not as a means to an end beyond the immediate gratification which it brings. (To describe an activity as a form of play is not, of course, to denigrate it.) The fact that listening, and still more viewing, normally take place at home means that they are associated with doing-what-you-like rather than with doing-what-you-must. The 'home' where this is not so does not deserve the name. In fact, of course, listening is not 'for free' any more than is running water, but both feel free because the cost is neither collected at the time of consumption nor related to the amount consumed. These three elements constitute a frame of reference peculiar to listening and viewing. What distinguishes it from the frames of reference of other forms of leisure activity, such as going to the cinema, the concert hall, to church or to a football match, is that all three of its elements contribute to making it a relaxed, unceremonious activity, to be indulged in or refrained from with a minimum of fuss and no feeling of obligation towards the provider.

Add to this that it is natural and human, and in the final analysis probably biologically sensible, for man to seek his satisfactions with the minimum expenditure of effort. If you are only out to enjoy yourself, why do it the hard way? To respond to the kinds of demands which are pre-conditions of deriving satisfaction from some kinds of listening may well be considered 'the hard way'. Why should one go to the trouble of finding out about the nuances of greyhound racing, or about the way the Greeks thought of theatre if one does not think that, even then, watching dog-racing or listening to *Antigone* would be interesting? To be sure, greater satisfactions in listening may be within one's grasp if one is prepared to pay the price, but the price may not seem worth paying.

So, in the context of listening as play, at home and for free, the scales are heavily weighted against the demanding broadcast. While, of course, it is true that individuals may, and often do, change their ideas about the price they are prepared to pay for their satisfactions with the result that they widen their horizons of enjoyment, those who, in the bright dawn of broadcasting, saw it as a means by which the tastes of the public would be rapidly raised to hitherto undreamed-of heights seem to me to have woefully underestimated the weight of inertia to be overcome before there can be such a consummation.

In the light of the evidence that the more demanding a broadcast the smaller its audience was likely to be, some sadly over-simplified suppositions flourished about what were called Highbrows and Lowbrows. The notion was current thirty years ago that the listening population was pyramidal. At the top of the pyramid were the highbrows, the few really discriminating listeners; mostly well-educated, they were to be found in congeries in the (ancient) university cities, in Hampstead (but not West Hampstead), Highgate and perhaps Hazelmere but definitely not in Bermondsey, Beeston or Bootle. They were to be seen in the Wigmore Hall, at Little Revues and in select art shows in Cork Street; they read *The Times, The Guardian* and the posh Sundays.

The lowbrows, at the base of the pyramid, were the 'mass audience'. You didn't have to look for them, they were everywhere. They mostly listened to the Light Programme, though they would listen to the Home Service if it broadcast *Grand Hotel* from Eastbourne. Few of them had not left school on their fourteenth birthdays and they read *The News of the World, The People* and the *Mirror*. Of course they were splendid chaps who had been marvellous in the Blitz, but there was no denying that in terms of worthwhile broadcasting they were a total loss. Between these two extremes were a puzzling bunch of mid-brows – *Daily Express*-reading types – for whom there was perhaps some hope.

Perhaps this is an unfair caricature of the attitude I am describing. Some of those who accepted the pyramid-theory held diametrically opposite views about the relative merits of tip and base. But the theory did seem consistent with the evidence we were providing not only about the size, but also about the social composition of audiences for different kinds of broadcasts: the more demanding broadcasts were listened to by a much larger proportion of the upper middle class than of the working class, while the reverse was true of the least demanding programmes. For example, the audience of Obey's *Noah* and of *Dick Barton: Special Agent* had diametrically opposite social class 'profiles'. *Noah* was heard by 20 per cent of the upper middle class, 14 per cent of the lower middle class and 9 per cent of the working class, whereas *Dick Barton*'s audience included 9 per cent of the upper middle class, 14 per cent of the lower middle class and 20 per cent of the working class.

This kind of thinking wilted in the fifties thanks to the social changes in Britain and to the influence of such writers as Richard Hoggart (*The Uses of Literacy*). But we were able to show by supplementary studies that the pyramid-theory was inadequate because it failed to take account of all the facts. The most striking demonstration of this was provided by a study of the patronage of the Third Programme. We found that, far from confining their listening to the Third Programme, most of those who valued it and listened to it frequently nevertheless spent more time in listening to the other services, the Home Service and the Light Programme.

While there may have been people who fitted the highbrow-lowbrow stereotypes, there was in fact widespread catholicity in listening. A liking for light music, comedy shows and football commentaries tended to be common to all levels of brow. What usually distinguished the so-called highbrow from the lowbrow was not that he disliked easy fare but that he also liked other kinds. He did not perhaps listen to undemanding material as much as the lowbrow did because he liked a more varied diet, but listen to, and enjoy it, he certainly did. The archetypal lowbrow confined his listening to the undemanding; the archetypal highbrow experienced moods when he was as ready for easily assimilated entertainment as the next man.

There was also differences between the age-composition of audiences which had less bearing on the pyramid theory. There were comparatively few types of programme which drew audiences with an age-composition totally at variance with that of the listening public as a whole, and these few were predictable. For example, young people figured out of all proportion in the audiences for dance music. Apart from such special cases, the older the listener the greater the likelihood that he would listen to the more demanding material, or more precisely, would be more catholic and include it amongst the programmes he listened to. In so far as this kind of behaviour reflected open-mindedness, a willingness to experiment or a relative freedom from the shackles of habit it might have been expected that the young rather than their elders would exhibit it. Against this it might be argued that catholicity is fostered by experience and hence would be an attribute of age. But it seems more probable that the explanation was a relatively simple one: that the role of broadcasting tended to change with age.

Today, when the demands of teenagers are catered for far more assiduously than they were thirty years ago, it is a matter of common observation that radio's role for many young people seems to be very restricted indeed – they look to it for pop music and little else. (It is equally obvious that the passion for pop does not usually last, so that the turnover of the pop public is rapid.) Radio may well have had an equally restricted role for young people in the pre-pop, pre-TV, age though much less was done to cater for it.

It is my opinion that the roles which listening and viewing play in people's lives tend to multiply as they get older. For instance, adolescents like to spend their leisure with their peers, out of sight of the possibly censorious scrutiny of their parents, hence for them radio's role as a way of passing the time at home is far less than it will be when evenings have to be spent at home because of the babies upstairs or, at a later stage, when going out in the evening does not seem to be worth the trouble. The tendency for catholicity in listening and viewing to increase as people get older may simply be a result of changing circumstances.

To return to the narrative: by the time the war in Europe ended Audience Research was very different from what it had been when the war began. The panels had been reflecting listeners' reactions to broadcasts for two and a half years and the HLCs had been at work even longer. The Survey of Listening had been running for four and a half years for the last two of which we had had our own field-force of interviewers. We had recruited a remarkable woman to set it up: Winifred M. Gill. She had been at the Slade and had worked with Roger Fry in the Omega Workshops before World War I. Later she had taken up social work and when I first met her was Sub-Warden of the Bristol University Settlement. In the Spring of 1939 we had commissioned her to produce an impressionistic study of the impact of broadcasting on a working class area of Bristol. She wrote a vivid and perceptive report which the BBC published as a pamphlet entitled *Broadcasting and Everyday Life*. Unfortunately it first saw the light on the day World War II broke out and so, not surprisingly, passed unnoticed by the Press.

Among her other accomplishments Winifred Gill was a skilled toy-maker, puppeteer and mimic. Memorable snatches of conversation in public places had a way of occurring when she was within ear-shot, as when on the top of a bus during the V1 bombardment of London she overheard one woman say to another 'And d'you know dear, the flying-bomb come and blew off all 'er clothes except 'er corset-belt!' at which her companion exclaimed in horror 'Oh! I don't wear one!'

But VE Day was no time for taking breath. It had been decided that the BBC's domestic services should assume their peace-time shape with a minimum of delay. By the beginning of August 1945 the Light Programme would replace the General Forces Programme and Home Service would revert to being a federation of regional services – Scottish, North, Midlands, Wales, West and Northern Ireland – with a basic Home Service planned in London on which each of these could draw. There was to be a Third Programme, though this would not start for a further year, and the Television Service was to begin again on the day when Victory was formally celebrated in June 1946.

These changes involved Audience Research in a radical re-adaptation and expansion of its services. On the audience measurement side estimates of listening on a national scale would no longer be adequate. There would also have to be estimates of listening in each region. That meant that instead of interviewing each day a single sample to represent the population of Great Britain we should have to interview a separate sample in each region, each big enough to give reliable results by itself. (Their findings would be combined to give national data, due weight, of course, having been given to the differing regional populations.) We decided to make each regional sample 600 and this meant that – since at first we omitted Northern Ireland – we were committed to making 3,600 interviews a day instead of 800 as we had done up till then. The task of increasing the pool of available interviewers was prodigious. Possible candidates had to be found and the best of them selected and trained. But Winifred Gill and her staff did the job and were ready when the day, August 1st, came.

Re-organisation of the Listening Panels presented a different kind of problem. Previously they had been organised in terms of output with separate Panels for Music, Talks, Plays, Features and Light Entertainment. Now there had to be regional panels for it would have been wasteful to send the same questionnaires to everyone since many Home Service programmes would be confined to one or two regions. As it would have been impossibly complicated to have had five output panels for each of five regions we scrapped this form of organisation altogether. Instead, we set up six panels, one for each region and each with 600 members making 3,600 in all. Half of each regional panel, chosen at random, was told they belonged to Section A and half to Section B. The qualifications for membership were simply residential – listeners' tastes no longer come into it – we tried as far as we could to make each Panel representative of the regional public in terms of age, sex and educational level.

In other respects the operation closely resembled its pre-war predecessor. There was the same injunction not to 'duty-listen', panel members being asked to return only the questionnaires relating to the broadcasts they listened to in the ordinary course. We speeded things up by distributing questionnaires and asking for them back twice a week instead of only once. And the other change was the substitution, referred to in Chapter 7, of an alphabetical scale for summing up reactions to replace marks-out-of-ten.

We continued to recruit panel members by voluntary enlistment, making our needs known by announcements over the air and in the *Radio Times*. We had far more applicants than we needed. We would send each of them a detail form on which they would tell us about themselves. Then, with a specification of our needs at hand, we would fill the vacancies and ask those not chosen to stand by as a reserve. We found it best not to specify a fixed term of service. Some panel members would quickly tire and drop out while others would give faithful service over long periods. Tests showed that the length of service made no appreciable difference to panel members' reactions to the programmes they heard.

Later, when television gradually supplanted radio as the public's primary source of broadcasting, recruitment for the Listening Panels became more difficult in the smaller regions, though never in London and the North. When Northern Ireland was added to the six British regions, keeping its Panel up to strength was a labour of Sisyphus.

One characteristic of post-war listening which we had not foreseen and hence had not anticipated in planning the Panels' operation was that the gap between the size of the audiences of the popular shows and those of minority programmes would widen considerably. With hindsight it is easy to see why this happened. Released from wartime obligations and with more channels available, it was possible for the BBC to devote time to more recondite material and to material for numerically restricted groups. We knew this was happening, of course, but neither we nor, I think, the Corporation as a whole, expected audiences for these broadcasts to be quite as small as they were. The Third Programme was the classic case. When it first started substantial numbers of people listened to it but many of them evidently did so simply out of curiosity for its audiences soon fell sharply; very soon there was typically only one person listening to the Third Programme for every ninety-nine listening to the Home and Light. There is no doubt that this caused disappointment inside the Corporation but it did not shake its belief that the introduction of the Third Programme had been fully justified. It was felt that since the BBC transmitted with two services offering less esoteric fare, its third could legitimately be a Third.

The problem with which this confronted Audience Research's Panel operation arose from the fact that, if panel members did as they were bid and only returned questionnaires for the broadcasts they would have listened to anyway, we could legitimately expect the number to be returned for any programme to be related to the size of its audience. If the audience was very small, this number would be alarmingly few. Thus if we sent out a questionnaire about a Third Programme broadcast which had an audience amounting to 0.2 per cent of the population, we were only entitled to expect similar proportion of panel members to return them and that would have meant only seven completed questionnaires. In practice we would get a good deal more because, in the nature of things, panel members tended to listen more than did the general public, but even so we found that the numbers of questionnaires returned for Third Programme broadcasts were quite inadequate to form the basis of reports.

This called for action so we decided to set up a separate Third Programme Panel consisting of people who were 'patrons' of the Third. To be classed as a patron did not mean that a person must listen to the Third exclusively but simply that he was 'in the market' for it. Thus there was no place in this Panel for listeners to whom the Third Programme was a closed book – and that ruled out the vast majority of the population. There was no difficulty about recruiting this Panel; all we had to do was to make it known in the Third Programme itself. It had a thousand members and this proved quite enough to ensure that we received an adequate number of completed questionnaires.

The need which the Panels were set up to satisfy – for something equivalent to the response of the audience in the theatre which could be set alongside our equivalent of the box office – was also felt in the temple of commercial broadcasting, the U.S.A. In my first visit there after the war, in September 1947, I saw their answer in operation. It was a device known after its progenitors as the Stanton-Lazarsfeld Programme Analyser. It involved bringing an audience into a studio to hear a recording of a broadcast. Each member of the audience was given a pair of push-buttons, a green (positive) and a red (negative). They were told to push the green button when they experienced pleasure and the red when they experienced pain, though it was not quite put like that. The buttons activated a pair of needles which traced graphs, known as Programme Profiles, on a moving tape calibrated in minutes. A producer with strong nerves could sit by this instrument and watch the Profile of his show develop before his eyes. Its designers, however, stressed that the button-pushing was only a necessary preliminary to the important part of the study which was a group-interview in which the administrator of the session, with the Programme Profile in front of him, would endeavour to elicit from the audience their reasons for reacting in the way they had.

Since then Programme Analysers have become a great deal more sophisticated. For instance, instead of two push-buttons each guinea pig can now be given a single dial which enables him to express varying degrees of emotion. Like most new devices when first publicised, the Programme Analyser came in for a good deal of lay derision. To be sure, it was an easy target, though just why it should be more risible than claps and boos is difficult to see. In any event, its value depended on how intelligently it was used and that it could be used intelligently was hardly in doubt.

Later, a substantial business in testing commercials was built up by the Schwerin Corporation which, paradoxically, dispensed with the mechanical element altogether. In their test sessions the audience would run to hundreds. Each individual would be given a sheet of paper with numbers running down the left-hand side. At pre-arranged moments during a playback bold numbers would be thrown on a screen and the assembled guinea-pigs would be required to record either a pro or a con vote against the appropriate number on their sheet of paper. When the playback finished the sheets of paper would be collected and the Profile compiled from a quick clerical count.

In one form or another the technique of recording audiences' reactions to programmes *as they listened to them* was a valuable addition to audience research's toolbag, to be used when appropriate. In some respects, particularly in the simultaneity, it was superior to the panel method but it could never have replaced it, if only for administrative reasons. The panel method was flexible and economical enough to yield material about a very large number of programmes every week whereas the programme analyser method, involving as it did bringing people into studios, could never have been employed on a comparable scale.

The audience reaction side of the department's work had,

during its formative war-time years, been in Eric Mosely's charge and when he left to join the National Dock Labour Corporation, I knew I would have a job to find anyone of similar calibre to replace him. But luck was on my side. It was the time when BBC staff who had been absent on war-service were being re-settled. All established staff had been promised re-settlement, but it wasn't always possible to give them back the precise jobs they had had before – nor was this always what they wanted; more than one lift boy was demobbed as a full colonel.

One of the returning warriors was a man I had known well personally – Joe Trenamen. Before the war he had been a seller of advertising space for *The Listener*, but it was obvious to his friends that his talents were being wasted. During his service in the Royal Army Education Corps he had done a remarkable job in developing methods of teaching illiterate young delinquents to read. This work was subsequently published as *Out of Step: A Study of Young Delinquents in Wartime* (Methuen). I give the Army full marks for letting him have his head, even though they never got round to giving him a commission. His success was the result of a combination of gifts: a flair for research, for which he had no academic training, and for teaching and perhaps more important than either, a sensitivity about people which made it possible for him to empathise with young men who, though they usually were none too bright, were well aware that their inability to read would mean that society would not have much time for them.

I asked him if he would like to join our team when he was released and he jumped at the chance. The Resettlement Board, whose problems were more often those of finding the right niches where no right niches were immediately apparent, raised no difficulties. Joe was a remarkable man. In manner, and indeed in appearance, he was gentle. It came as no surprise to learn that he was a Morris-dancer and a bird-watcher, that he had artistic gifts and was, in his spare-time, a Prison-visitor. But he had an impressive vein of toughness and sheer persistence. Once he had decided to enter the field of social research, he quietly determined that he would be no amateur.

Though already over 30, with the responsibilities of a wife and family, he set about educating himself, first by taking a degree in social science and later a doctorate. He was something of a loner; so though we were sad, we were not really surprised when after a few years in audience research he moved over to being the BBC's first Further Education Officer. There he could cultivate a new field more or less on his own. Some years later he left the BBC for academic life as the first Granada Television Fellow at Leeds University where he published, jointly with D. McQuail, *Television and the Political Image* (Methuen, 1960) and *Television and Politics: Its Uses and Influence* (Faber & Faber, 1965). Joe's premature death from cancer left a yawning gap in the world of social research and an unfillable void in the hearts of his friends. His doctorate thesis, *Communication and Comprehension,* was posthumously published by Longmans, Green in 1967.

9 P. & D.

In the ordinary course the BBC's second Charter would have expired in 1946, but Parliament decided to extend it for five years since so much of its currency, 1936–46, had been years of war. Well in advance of the new expiry date Lord Beveridge was nominated to chair a Committee of Inquiry to review the BBC's performance and make recommendations about its future. Beveridge was said to be determined to find *something* wrong with an organisation which he thought, as did a good many others, had been showered with a great deal more praise than was good for it. Naturally Haley, then D-G, took a very lively interest in the preparation of the BBC's evidence, brilliantly directed by Maurice Farquharson.

I was asked to prepare two documents. One would describe the methods we used and the other would be a wide-ranging review of our findings. The first of the two eventually appeared *in toto* in the Committee's Volume II, *The Evidence*, but it was the second which, I think, Haley was the more pleased with. He saw it as a contribution to softening up the old man by tickling his statistical pallet. Be that as it may, when the Committee's report finally appeared, it did not criticise the methods we used. It said: 'Broadcasting authorities cannot serve the public without studying it: they must study it deliberately ... if audience research is worth doing at all, it is worth doing well. For broadcasting without study of the audience is dull dictation, it is not responsible public service.'

At this time the Chairman of the BBC was Lord Simon of Wythenshawe. Physically imposing, florid and never to be seen without a deep starched collar, he was something of a butt for the BBC wits. Admittedly his methods of 'keeping in touch' were a little bizarre. From time to time he would send for one for a 'chat' and produce a file in which, the theory was, were his notes of the previous conversation, but as he frequently forgot to keep them up to date, at each encounter one had a feeling of *déja vu*.

Lady Simon – who, when the Simons joined the Labour Party, startled the good Labour Women of Manchester by insisting that they should call her Shena – evidently thought that her husband's appointment as Chairman of the BBC entitled her to a role in its activities. This might have been acceptable had it not taken the forms it did. My own experience of her interpretation of her role was certainly disconcerting. Without telling me, she summoned a member of my staff, with whom she had some previous slight acquaintance, to tea at the Simon flat at Marsham Court and then proceeded to question her about her boss.

I liked Lord Simon and I had reason to be grateful to him. He genuinely cared about audience research and I believe he had a great deal to do with an important step which had far-reaching effects.

I had become increasingly concerned about the way the BBC's budgeting system affected us. We were given an annual global sum to cover the services we were providing but this left very little margin for *ad hoc* studies or experiments in methods. Experiments were essential – audience research couldn't stand still – and the need to undertake studies which fell outside the range of our continuous audience measurements and assessments of audience reaction was daily becoming more apparent. What little margin we had had constantly to be eaten into by the need to improve the functioning of the Survey of Listening and the Panels. By a lucky break I was able to bring this forcibly to the notice of the Governors.

George (later Sir George) Barnes lit the fuse. I first came to know him when he was Head of Talks. A donnish type, he was chosen as the first Controller of the Third Programme and in that capacity I came to know him better and like him more. Then he was elevated to a new post with the somewhat risible title of Director of the Spoken Word. This carried a seat on the Board of Management of which the D-G was the Chairman and which was the top executive committee of the Corporation.

Soon after he was appointed, George suggested that the time was ripe to get an outside expert to look at, and report on, the Corporation's Audience Research Department. This seemed to me to be a very understandable and sensible suggestion. Audience Research was now ten years old, the form it had taken and the methods it used were pretty well entirely what I had suggested if only because there hadn't been anyone else in the BBC in a position to say I was wrong. If the Corporation did not feel too happy with this situation, neither did I.

So when Haley told me the Board of Management had agreed to George's suggestion – but that I was not to take this as an implied criticism – I said I welcomed it. The next problem was to find the 'outside expert'. That was easier said than done because, since the BBC was a monopoly, nobody else had any experience of conducting audience research in this country. I suggested that market research was the nearest analogous field. The Corporation agreed, but was still stuck because this wasn't a field with which they were acquainted. The slightly ludicrous consequence was that I was asked to suggest someone and the obvious choice, as the outstanding figure in market research at the time, was my old friend Mark Abrams! In recommending that he be the inquisitor I made no secret of our long friendship but this didn't prevent my nomination from being accepted.

Mark duly reported. He pointed to some weak spots but they were an almost exact recapitulation of those to which I had myself repeatedly called attention as things which could not be put right without further funds and staff. In passing on Mark's report I didn't hesitate to plug this point hoping that if they didn't believe me, they would believe him. The report, with my comments, reached the D-G's desk a few days before I was due to leave for a routine trip to America. It was typical of Haley that he made sure that before I left I got a message that he 'accepted' both documents.

Haley must have talked the matter over with Simon while I was away. The outcome was a memo from Haley, historic for Audience Research, which invited me to say how I would spend an annual grant of £10,000 'ear-marked for *ad hoc* enquiries and experiments'. The grant, if it were made, would come up for review each year. Its great virtue would be that it could not be diverted to meet the greedy needs of our existing services. If Simon had had a hand in this, his name shall be for ever blessed.

My answer evidently satisfied the Board for the grant came through. I decided to set up a Projects and Developments Section within the department. The disciplines it would call upon were obviously statistics and psychology. The choice of statistician was no problem. While I had been in hospital wrestling with temporary blindness, Fred Littman had taken on a young mathematician, Brian Emmett, as a general assistant. He had served in R.A.F. Operational Research during the war and, it so happened, had been a Third Programme Panel member. With some of the characteristics of a wild Irishman (one of his forebears was Robert Emmett) Brian was, and is, an extremely able statistician. (His professional qualities were soon widely recognised outside the BBC for he subsequently served for some years as Hon. Secretary of the Royal Statistical Society.) He is also a man of wide and deep musical interests, with a nimble intelligence, strong convictions and a lovable nature. Some twenty years later the Corporation, to my great satisfaction, agreed that on my retirement he should succeed me as Head of Audience Research.

Finding the right psychologist was another matter. Although we were none of us complete ignoramuses in this field, we were laymen and felt the need for authoritative guidance in an area in which there were a good many conflicting schools of thought. So we decided to set up an Advisory Committee of Psychologists. Alec Rodger, then Hon. Secretary of the British Psychological Society, consented to be Chairman. He was a reader at Birkbeck College and was well known for his work in developing Vocational Guidance. He helped choose the others. They were Sir Cyril Burt, the doyen of psychology in Britain, a benign figure then struggling courageously with increasing deafness; R. H. Thouless of Cambridge, a tousle-headed High Anglican whose side interests include para-psychology; Philip Vernon of London University, the outstanding expert on intelligence tests, a man of formidable intelligence himself but of almost paralysing shyness; Jack (W.J.H.) Sprott of Nottingham who had been a contemporary of George Barnes at Balliol and whose Chair at Nottingham was for some odd reason designated as of Philosophy; T. H. Pear of Manchester who had early shown a realisation that broadcasting might have some interest for academic psychologists; the gentle Denis Harding of Bedford College, a poet as well as psychologist, and Rex Knight of Aberdeen, a man of massive common sense and executive ability who was one of the brilliant group of psychologists under J. R. Reece who had been called in by the War Office during the war to develop better methods of officer-selection than asking potential officers whether they hunted, shot or fished.

The Committee had all-day meetings once a quarter. At its first I described the methods we currently used and the problems which I thought we ought to tackle. I hope I didn't show how over-awed I felt addressing so distinguished a group, but when I got to know them better I was astonished to learn that they too had felt over-awed. Apart from the value of their counsel, we came to look forward to the meetings as highly congenial occasions. Over lunch there would always be some hilarious anecdote as when Pear recalled the occasion when, at a High Table in Cambridge in the early days of broadcasting, he had been describing the work he had been doing on Voice and Personality. Someone further down the Table intervened with a question: 'Excuse me but I could not help hearing what you were saying. Have you by any chance published your results anywhere?' 'As a matter of fact', said Pear, 'I have – in the *Radio Times*.' There was a pained silence for a moment; 'Then I wonder', came the rejoinder, 'whether you would be so good as to let me know when they will appear in a rather more accessible publication?'

With the help of the Committee we eventually appointed a psychologist: William A. Belson from Australia. To some extent this was a leap in the dark for, as Belson was then in Australia, he and we had to take one another on trust. He proved to be man of demonic energy who didn't spare himself – or his subordinates – and was full of ideas to which he held with sometimes passionate intensity. On a personal level we got on well, but on a professional level our relationship wasn't always plain-sailing. I think some of the difficulty arose from the differences between the British and Australian cultures. He was, I think, a little suspicious of British 'smoothness'. What we would see as tact, he was inclined to see as a lack of forthrightness; what we would see as a necessary flexibility, he would see as a surrender of principle. I am sure, because he once said so, that he thought my personal loyalty to the BBC bordered on the fanatical and at times led me perilously near to intellectual dishonesty; to me some of his attitudes appeared near-paranoic. But there can be no denying that Bill made a contribution to the development of audience research which was very considerable indeed – and he said, and I am sure he meant it, that he felt he had learned a lot from us. His departure to become Head of the Survey Research Centre at the LSE after some years with us was a very real loss to the department, though it must be confessed that his erstwhile colleagues thereafter seemed less prone to ulcers.

We decided that the first major task which Projects and Developments (or P. & D. as we came to call it) should get down to, once Belson had joined us, should be concerned with Comprehensibility. To what extent did people who listened to BBC talks take in what was said? We chose as the field of inquiry *Topic for To-Night*, a series of short talks which nightly followed the *Ten o'clock News* in the Light Programme and were intended not to comment on, but to supply the background to, some item which had been in the *News*. Our aim was to discover how much of the information in these talks was actually conveyed to those who listened to them.

The method Belson devised involved bringing listeners to Broadcasting House in the evening, playing over to them a recording of a recent *Topic* and subsequently getting them to answer, in writing, a series of questions the correct answers to which had all been given in the *Topic* they had just had played over to them. They were also required to answer other questions about themselves and were to tackle a simple Intelligence Test together designed to give data which would make it possible to express the findings in such terms as age, sex, occupational level and broad differences in I.Q.

There were plenty of problems to be solved; how to find people to invite, bearing in mind that the population to be studied were those who normally listened to the Light Programme at this time of night; how to persuade them to come to Broadcasting House and to co-operate when they got there; how to prevent them from cribbing; how to sell them the idea of doing an intelligence test and, by no means least important, how to ensure that they went away happy, feeling that they had spent an 'interesting evening'.

As it would be clearly impractical to cope with more than a limited number, at the most fifty, people at a time and as for research purposes we needed a substantial number of cases, sessions had to be held several nights a week spread over a couple of months. Altogether over a thousand listeners were put through their paces. The job of administering the sessions was shared amongst the senior members of the department and I found I really enjoyed this work. First there was the business of welcoming and putting at their ease a heterogeneous bunch of people, looking slightly bewildered and sometimes a little apprehensive as they filed, often for the first time in their lives, into a BBC studio. Coffee and biscuits were served at once and while they munched one would explain the object of the exercise and the evening's procedure. Technicalities were clearly out of place, but we owed it to them to explain why their co-operation was important. Then came the play-back, followed by the comprehension test which, of course, was not distributed in advance. An 'About Yourself' questionnaire came next. Then came the administration of the Intelligence Test. Selling it was a bit tricky, but by this time people were pretty much at their ease and in fact we never had any serious difficulty. It was what is known as a Power Test; it consisted of forty questions and people had to answer as many of them as possible in the time allowed. All the questions took the same form – 'What should go in the place of the dot in this series : 2 4 6 8 . ?' The early items were about as simple as that but they became progressively more difficult until the fortieth item which was: A H I M O . (the answer will be found at the end of this Chapter).

That ended the research part of the session. We then invited the group to have their say and to put any questions or make any comments on broadcasting they liked, however critical. There was rarely any problem about getting started. The wily administrator didn't immediately try to answer a criticism but invited others to endorse or differ from what had been said. As often as not the ensuing argument made an *ex cathedra* answer superfluous. These discussion periods were always friendly, if repetitious to the administrator who had heard it all before at previous sessions; they were often salutary, for us as well as for the assembled listeners. The frequency with which the departing listeners thanked us for an interesting evening, when in fact we had shamelessly used them, almost made us feel guilty.

The report on the experiment showed that the average listener to *Topic for To-night* could only answer 28 per cent of the questions correctly; in other words, when he listened to *Topic* in what were undoubtedly highly propitious conditions, without distractions and with the expectation of being questioned about it, he was only able, immediately afterwards, to give the right answer to about one in four questions concerning the facts which it contained. To be sure some acquitted themselves much better and, as might be expected, the higher the listener's IQ and occupational status the higher his comprehension score was likely to be. But the talks weren't intended for Mensa members but for 'average listeners'; they were deliberately couched in terms which it was thought would meet their needs and they were delivered by experienced journalists who wrote every day for the same kind of public.

The trouble seemed to be of three kinds. First, there was an evident tendency for broadcasters to over-estimate listeners' background knowledge of the subject he was dealing with – to take it for granted that they were familiar with facts which actually were new to them. Second, the talks which fared least well were those where the listener was left to sort out the principal points for himself or where there was no obvious straightforward progression of ideas. (These might have been satisfactory had they been written for reading but as radio talks, which must be taken in first time or not at all, they fell short.) Third, there were vocabulary difficulties – broadcasters too often used words which their listeners simply did not understand.

It was not surprising that the findings of the inquiry were received with something less than ecstacy in some quarters. The redoubtable Mary Somerville, then Controller of Talks, turned over the job of evaluating the report to John Scupham, her scholarly Head of School Broadcasting. He submitted a closely argued critical paper, which at least showed that someone had taken the trouble to read the report with care. As I recall, his main argument was that Comprehensibility wasn't everything. But apart from the fact that we had never argued that it was, I couldn't for the life of me see how, if people didn't understand what they had heard, the other magical virtues of broadcasting could display themselves. In any case, what was so surprising about a finding that broadcasters weren't quite so clever as, without any experimental evidence whatever, they had assumed themselves to be?

Methodologically, the most important result of the inquiry was what it taught us about the use of groups in research – not least that the limits of their toleration in answering questions were far less constricted than we had dared to hope, provided that trouble were taken to explain what was wanted and why. Some kinds of inquiry could not have been undertaken at all had the group-session method not been available. The *Topic for To-Night* study was one, for it depended on getting people to listen to broadcasts under controlled conditions and answering questions about them immediately afterwards. It is just conceivable that this could have been done by taking tape-recorders into people's homes, but this would have been hopelessly cumbersome. Where it was necessary, as it sometimes was, for the guinea-pig listener to hear or see the broadcast *on transmission*, there was no alternative to using group-sessions.

As the years passed there were an increasing number of studies which involved showing people a television programme; sometimes it would be one which had been broadcast, sometimes one which was to be viewed on transmission and sometimes one which had not yet been publicly shown – a 'dummy-run'. The object of the study would not necessarily be to test the programme's comprehensibility, as in the *Topic* inquiry, but to study other aspects of its impact, such as its likely effects, if any, on viewers' attitudes. An early example, in

1954, was a study of a proposed documentary programme which had the wholly worthy intention of showing cases of industrial conflict in such a way as to bring home, both to men and management, that the other fellow had a reasonable case as well as trying to do something towards dispersing their stereotypes of each other. The findings of the study made rueful reading. Both sides and their sympathisers commended the programme as admirable in intention and effective in execution. The only trouble was that both sides ended up confirmed in their conviction that they were right and the other side was wrong, and both showed evidence of a blissful unawareness that the case of the other fellow had been voiced in the programme at all. It was a classic case of selective perception.

As an alternative to gathering information by personal interviews, group sessions have some important advantages. The foremost is that, once people have taken the trouble to come together in a group-session, they are perfectly ready, indeed they expect, to co-operate by answering questions for a substantial length of time – maybe a couple of hours. Long personal interviews in private homes can be arranged, and in some social surveys they do take place, but they are much more difficult to fix up and, of course, are very expensive. A skilled interviewer might well find himself lucky to have accumulated ten cases in a week, whereas in a group-session he could get through thirty to fifty cases in a single evening. What is more, the administration of the kinds of questionnaires and tests which would necessitate a one- or two-hour interview calls for considerable skill, much more than is needed for getting answers to a simple questionnaire requiring answers on a few matters of fact or superficial opinion. Interviewers of the necessary qualifications do not grow on mulberry bushes so that any means of conserving their efforts is essential. In the group-session, too, the business of answering takes place in circumstances which are much more under the research-worker's control – they come much nearer to the conditions of a psychological laboratory than is possible in an interview in the informant's front-room.

Why, it may well be asked, does anyone ever send interviewers out in the field if the data could be gathered so much more economically and efficiently in a group interview? The answer is simple. The great disadvantage of group-session method lies in the difficulty of achieving a satisfactory sample, in other words, of persuading the people needed actually to turn up. It is true that in a survey consisting of personal interviews in people's homes, there will always be some of the sample sought who won't play; a survey in which 90 per cent of the sample sought is actually interviewed has done very well. But a survey based on group-sessions which achieved a similar success-rate would be a miracle. It is obviously far easier for a person to find a good reason for not making a journey to a meeting-place and giving up a whole evening than for him to refuse a maybe quite flattering request to answer some questions, made by a personable interviewer on the door-step or in the street.

P. & D. learnt by experience that they could only expect about a quarter of the people whom they invited to a group-session actually to turn up on the night. But some kinds of people were readier to come than others. The most decisive variable was what the Census people call 'occupational level', but what in a less mealy-mouthed age would have been called social class. The highest turn-up rates were those of the Professional and Highly Skilled, the lowest those of the Unskilled. Age was a factor too, but a less influential one, the 16–20-year-olds and the 50–60s tending to lag behind other age-groups. Other fascinating correlations were subsequently revealed by other research workers, though the significance of some of these may seem a trifle academic – such as that people who had lived in the same district a long time and had a 'Mum' living nearby tended *not* to turn up.

The bias introduced into the sample by these variable turn-up rates could to some extent be corrected by deliberately inviting more of the groups who had a low turn-up rate; more, that is, than their numbers in the population warranted. And, of course, it was also possible to adjust the findings by a process of 'weighting' at the analysis stage. (For example, if the Unskilled constituted only 10 per cent of the sample questioned when, to be properly represented, they should have constituted

30 per cent then the contribution of each of them would be given a weight of three.)

In the final analysis, however, there was always the haunting possibility that an unidentified Something was differentiating the acceptors from the refusers; something which, by being correlated with the subject being studied, would to an unknown degree invalidate generalisations drawn from the finding of the study. This, of course, is the old spectre Volunteer Bias in a different guise.

P. & D. was certainly not besotted by the group-session method. Its policy was to use whatever methods seemed best suited to the problem to be solved. When conventional personal interviews were made with samples of the population, they were not necessarily confined to questions asked and answered there and then. For example, when it was necessary to bring up-to-date our picture of the way the public spent its waking hours, the people called upon were asked to keep records of their behaviour over a week on specially prepared Diary forms which were collected eight days later. Sometimes questionnaires were sent by post and much experiment went into discovering ways of maximising the proportion returned. (The use of postal questionnaires was particularly appropriate where the sample was widely scattered, making interviewing prohibitive because of travelling costs. Inquiries about Farming programmes were often carried out in this way.)

A wide variety of questioning techniques were employed, some drawn from the quiver of experimental psychology and some specially created. The simple interrogatory form, which is basically conversational, may be perfectly adequate for many purposes but is not always so. Sometimes it is more effective to invite people to examine a series of statements made by other people like themselves and invite them to indicate the one with which they find themselves most nearly in agreement. (There is always a temptation, when this method is used, for the research worker to think up the statements himself. This can be dangerous. What people *really* say about an issue is often surprisingly different from what the research worker *thinks* they say.)

One useful form of inquiry is basically spatial. The

informant will be asked to consider a layout in which adjectives are opposed to one another like this:

interesting	☐	☐	☐	☐	☐	dull
simple	☐	☐	☐	☐	☐	complicated
kind	☐	☐	☐	☐	☐	cruel
foolish	☐	☐	☐	☐	☐	wise

He will then be asked to consider each pair and to indicate, by putting a tick in the appropriate square, just how interesting/dull, simple/complicated, kind/cruel, etc., he thought the subject being studied was. The biggest problem in this form of enquiry is that of ensuring that the opposing adjectives really are, and will be seen as being, antitheses.

One of the earliest projects carried out by P. & D. was a study of the market for the Third Programme. We wanted to try to discover whether the people the Third's planners visualised as constituting their target audience were, or were not, in fact its listeners. (This posed a sampling problem. In order to examine this question it would be necessary to question a sample of the whole population. But since we knew that most of the people so interviewed would turn out to be neither listeners to, nor by any stretch of imagination in the market for, the Third Programme, it would have been highly expensive to have carried out a national survey for this purpose alone. We solved this problem by seizing the opportunity of adding questions about our subject to a national survey we were conducting for different purposes.)

The research design required that we should eventually classify each person interviewed in terms of (a) the *likelihood* that he/she would listen to the Third if the planners' concept of their potential customers were well-grounded and (b) the frequency with which he did in fact listen to it.

The first step in devising a way of classifying people's potentiality as customers for the Third involved the planners themselves. It was for them to spell out precisely who they had in mind as their target audience in terms of characteristics about which information could be obtained in interviews. Four characteristics were agreed upon: (a) the informant's educational level; (b) his interest in a specified range of subjects with which the Third Programme frequently dealt; (c) his reading of any of a range of publications of a degree of sophistication similar to that of the Third Programme and (d) his intelligence level. The first three would be easy to establish in an interview. As to intelligence level, Belson had already carried out research which showed that this could be inferred, in very broad terms, from the informant's age and occupational level taken in combination.

Once we had these data, we could use them to assign each informant to one of four categories: Good, Fair, Poor, and Very Poor Prospects for the Third Programme. Decisions had to be made about what combinations of the four characteristics should qualify informants for particular categories. This job was assigned to a panel of independent judges who fortunately showed a high measure of agreement. When the results of the study were ultimately analysed in these terms, it was found that 2 per cent of the adult population fell into the Good Prospects category, 8 per cent were Fair, 20 per cent were Poor and 70 per cent were Very Poor Prospects for the Third Programme.

The data collected about frequency of listening was not confined to the Third Programme; people were asked about their listening to the other services as well. This made it possible to disguise the prime intention of these questions which, had it been apparent, might have led to exaggerated claims about Third Programme listening.

The study revealed that just under 5 per cent of the population were 'patrons' of the Third Programme, if a patron be defined as one who claimed to listen to it at least once a week. While there certainly was a relationship between being a patron and qualifying as a Prospect, the planners' conception of their market proved to be no more than partially correct. Thus only 26 per cent of the Good Prospects and 18 per cent of the Fairs turned out to be patrons, but so did 9 per cent of the Poor, and 3 per cent of the Very Poor, Prospects. Thus a substantial proportion of the actual patrons of the Third were drawn from the ranks of those whom the planners did not consider as promising prospects for it.

There were two incidental findings of this study which were of particular interest. One of them has already been referred to; it effectively disposed of a prevailing idea that the Third Programme listener was a race apart, listening to the Third and nothing else: even the most assiduous of them actually spent more time listening to the other services than they did to the Third. The other concerned the attitude to the Third Programme of that great majority of the population who never dreamed of listening to it: comparatively few of them opposed its existence, far more approved of it – if only because it ensured that 'a lot of high-brow stuff would no longer clutter-up the Home and Light'.

Many of P. & D.'s studies related to specific broadcasts (or series of broadcasts) either already, or yet to be, transmitted. Two have been referred to above: *Topic for To-night* and *Management and Men*. The initiative in these cases normally came from the producer. He might want to know what assumptions he should make about his audience's knowledgeability and their existing attitudes towards the subject he was to deal with. For example, when Christopher Mayhew was preparing a television series on *Race Relations in Africa* he asked us to find out how far his probable viewers would be acquainted with the facts of the case and – if they had any sympathies – where these sympathies lay.

We would sometimes be asked to pre-test putative programmes, providing the department concerned with a picture of their likely reception by the public. On other occasions our terms of reference would relate to the broadcast's effects; whether it achieved some specific objective which had been set for it; whether there had been any unintended side-effects or, more generally, what effects it did produce over and above those of interesting and entertaining its audience which our normal machinery for assessing audience reaction could be relied upon to reveal.

In the nature of things we could not do more than measure the *immediate* effects of broadcasts, i.e. those which occurred within at most a day or two of its being transmitted. The measurement of the *long-term* effects of individual broadcasts eluded us, if for no other reason than that – if there were any – they would be likely to be hopelessly entangled with effects of other factors like the subsequent reading of newspapers or conversations with friends. In any case though no doubt individual broadcasts do sometimes cause indentifiable long-term effects, such cases must be very rare indeed.

Useful and salutary though the study of the immediate effects of a broadcast can be, it would be a mistake to expect that an accumulation of such studies would add up to an adequate assessment of the full effect of broadcasting on society for this is a case where the whole is greater than the sum of its parts. It is pertinent here to mention that ambitious projects for the study of the general effects of television and radio which take these media as their starting point and then seek for the effects which their consumption produces are now out-of-favour amongst research workers. There is an increasing recognition that there is something rather artificial about this approach.

Nowadays viewing television – and listening to radio – are seen as merely two of the many means which people use to gratify their social and psychological needs. There are many other means such as social intercourse, reading newspapers, magazines and books, going to the cinema, to church or to a football match, digging the garden and exploring the countryside. People's psychological needs are, of course, also varied. To name only some, there is the need for information (from 'Has Ernie picked my number?' 'What won the 2.30?' and 'Is it going to rain today?' to 'What exactly is DNA?'); there is the need for reassurance (that I am not isolated, that our leaders can be trusted, that life does make some kind of sense); the need for relaxation (in laughter, in fantasy or in vicarious experience) and, not least, there is the need to reduce loneliness.

It is now seen as more realistic, when studying the relationship between individuals and the broadcasting media, to start with people and ask what they do with the media rather than starting with the broadcasting media and then asking what they 'do to' people. More precisely this means first identifying the needs which people feel they must satisfy and then finding out which particular means, including viewing and listening, they choose in their search for the satisfaction of each particular need. (This way of seeing the problem is known as the 'Uses and Gratifications Approach'.)

Other P. & D. inquiries examined particular types of output. For example, shortly after the Suez affair the Board of Management asked us to make a thorough study of *The News*. This involved not only an exhaustive examination of audience statistics to show how much the various bulletins were listened to by different sections of the population and the extent to which the audiences for different bulletins consisted of the same people. It also involved a survey to establish the public standing of the BBC News Service relative to that of the press in terms of interestingness and trustworthiness and how reliable, clear, impartial and topical it was thought to be. People were also asked how they used each bulletin, about the way the news was read and whether they thought more, or less, time should be devoted to news about sport, crime, royalty, foreign affairs and home politics. This was supported by group sessions in which over 1,100 members of the public took part by listening to news bulletins in the studio and subsequently answering questions about each item. (This study was repeated some six years later.)

The broadcasting of music was the subject of a whole series of inquiries. The musical tastes of the population as a whole were studied in 1963, the public for serious music in 1964, tastes in Light Music in 1967 and the attitudes and opinions of listeners to the Music Programme (which then filled the daytime hours of what is now Radio 3) in 1969. Religious broadcasting was studied in rather a different way. The Religious Broadcasting Department, backed by what everyone knew as CRACK (The Central Religious Advisory Committee) wanted to know the extent to which they were, or were not, preaching to the converted. So we devised a questionnaire about religious beliefs and practices (including listening to religious broadcasts) and arranged for the fieldwork to be done by the Gallup Poll (we felt that some people might wonder why the BBC was asking them whether they believed in God and an after-life). The findings were printed for distribution to religious leaders and other interested parties as *Religious Broad-*

casting and the Public, 1955. It fell to me to attend a meeting of CRACK when the report was finished and I recall being impressed by the spectacle of Protestant and Catholic leaders working together in obvious cordiality – a sight which was less common then than it is today.

Other projects had as their subjects particular types of 'consumer' such as the farming community, the blind or the population of the Highlands and Islands of Scotland. One of the most ambitious of these was a study of minors. It originated from producers charged with providing programmes for adolescents but soon broadened out into the much more extensive exercise of providing a picture of the population from 5 to 20, their viewing and listening facilities (and how much they used them), their leisure interests and their patterns of activity on weekdays and at weekends. Since minors are anything but a homogeneous group, separate results had to be prepared to 5–7s, 8–11s, 12–15s and 16–20-year-olds.

The successful completion of this study encouraged us to look again at the question of extending the scope of the daily Survey of Listening and Viewing to include children. From its beginning in 1939 its lower age limit had been 16. Everyone would have welcomed information about children's listening but the problems involved in gathering it seemed at the time insuperable. After the war, and even more after the revival of television, the exclusion of children came to be seen as not only illogical but increasingly intolerable. Devising a plan and carrying out the necessary experiments fell squarely in the lap of P. & D. so the project was remitted to Emmett.

With characteristic vigour and freshness of approach he was able to demonstrate that questioning children about their previous day's listening and viewing was no more difficult, indeed in some ways it was easier, than questioning adults. There was no reason to think that the results would be less reliable; children, on the whole, were clearer about what they had heard than their parents were. A rather different approach was needed; the parents' permission would always have to be sought and, with the youngest children, some parental help would have to be admitted; a specially trained group of women interviewers would have to be employed and different techniques of sample selection applied.

We came to the conclusion that if Emmett's recommendations were followed the lower age limit of the Survey could be fixed at 5, the daily sample of adults being stretched to include 15-year-olds and augmented by 300 5–7s, 400 8–11s and 300 12–14-year-olds. Our plan was accepted and put into effect in 1960 – it all went so smoothly that in retrospect we wondered why it had seemed so daunting in anticipation.

The answer to the problem on page 140 is that, in the series A H I M O . the full stop stands for T for this is the next letter in the alphabet which is unchanged if looked at in a mirror.

10 Television: The Last Years of the Monopoly

The BBC Television service which, when it opened in the autumn of 1936, had been the world's first public television service, had been abruptly shut down on the outbreak of the war. It re-opened in June 1946 – on the day when Victory was formally celebrated with eminently telegenic parades. But its coverage was limited to the range of the Alexandra Palace transmitter and even in that area its potential audience was very small. No one knew how many sets there were when the service went off the air in September 1939. It wasn't until after the war, when the viewer was required to take out a 'combined sound and television' licence, that the GPO could issue firm figures. Nine months after the resumption of the service there were still less than 15,000.

However, no one doubted that the number would increase rapidly – as it had done in the U.S.A. in the forties. In the event the rate of increase far outstripped that of radio in its formative years. At first a luxury, the television set became increasingly to be regarded as a necessity. There was a ten-fold increase in the first two years and in four years there were a hundred TV licences for every one on re-opening day. There were six million by 1956 and ten million by 1960. By the middle of the sixties virtually every household in the U.K. had its television receiver.

Maurice Gorham was the first post-war head of Television, with Cecil McGivern as his head of Programmes. Maurice, a genial burly Irishman distinguished for his total obliviousness to cold in the bitterest weather together with an encyclopaedic knowledge of London pubs and seemingly inexhaustible capacity for consuming beer but being unaffected by it, had previously been Editor of the *Radio Times* and later head of the Light Programme. He was a convert to audience research and had all the convert's enthusiasm for his new faith. He was insistent that audience research should serve television as soon as possible. Cecil, who had been a radio feature producer of distinction, supported him but realised that in the first year or two there wasn't much that audience research could contribute. In those early days it was as much as all the tiny staff at Alexandra Palace could do to find and produce enough programmes to fill the limited transmission hours at the same time as they recruited and trained staff to put the programmes on the air. As McGivern said of his job, 'Just to keep it going is a headache'.

Between us we decided that the Television Service would need the same kind of continuous audience research service as was already being provided for radio, viz. measurements of consumption programme by programme and assessments of audiences' reactions to the programmes they saw. We would also have to be ready to undertake such *ad hoc* inquiries as might be required. Audience measurement, we decided, could best be provided by extending the scope of our daily survey to include TV programmes so that it became a Survey of Listening *and Viewing*. But this would not be practicable while TV audiences were very small for they would barely show up in our samples of the whole population. It would also be some time, though not so long, before we could set up a Viewing Panel, comparable to our Listening Panels, to gather information about audiences' reactions.

A series of *ad hoc* studies was planned. Three were carried through in the pre-ITV period, the first in 1948, the second in 1950 and the third in 1954. They set out to discover what kinds of people were becoming viewers, how much they were viewing, and how the way they spent their leisure hours was being affected – in particular how the possession of a television set was affecting radio listening habits.

In the first two inquiries we drew our samples of viewing families, with the ready co-operation of the GPO, from the current lists of television licence holders. In the 1948 inquiry the sample was 1,000, but in the 1950 inquiry it was 3,000 for we had to ensure that veteran viewers, by then a dwindling band, were adequately represented. Our interviewers had two tasks: first to gather certain basic information about each family and secondly to persuade each family to accept and complete a specially designed 'log-book'. This was divided into quarter-hours with columns for various kinds of activity such as viewing, listening, having a meal, doing household chores, and visiting the cinema. To provide Control groups, interviewers were told to call at the house next door (or the nearest neighbour without a television set) and go through the same routine. We hoped in this way to be able to compare our samples of viewers with comparable samples of non-viewers. The assumption behind this plan was that, in the matter of housing in South-East England, birds of a feather would have flocked together. (In the event it turned out that neighbouring families were more likely to resemble one another in terms of education than in terms of income.)

The 1954 inquiry was based on several sources. By then our daily Survey was yielding information about the public's current viewing but we conducted a special interview survey to yield us additional information about, for example, leisure habits. The television sample included 1,300, and the Control group 1,200, adults. In addition we were able to draw on the findings of a study of the 5–20-year-old population which we had conducted in 1953 and in which information was collected about 3,700 young people.

The findings showed that television was rapidly spreading downwards through the social pyramid. At the end of 1947 the 'top' 12 per cent of the population owned 48 per cent of all the television sets; six years later their share was down to 18 per cent. During the same period the 'bottom' two-thirds increased their share of the total from 25 to 45 per cent. There was still some way to go before television ownership was spread evenly throughout the population but this was clearly only a matter of time.

These were the days when intellectual snobbery about television was still rife. *The Observer* carried Marghanita Laski's list of the commonest rationalisations for having fallen for a TV set. Under the headline 'We've got a television set because . . .' it included, if my memory is to be relied on, '. . . my old parents like it,' '. . . they watch it in the kitchen,' '. . . the children wanted it'. Certainly the inquiries showed that given two neighbouring middle-class families of similar income, but differing educational levels, the one with the lower educational level would be more likely to have television.

The inquiries left no doubt about the appetite for viewing among those who had acquired television sets. Typically, in 1954 over 40 per cent of the television sample would be viewing at any given moment during the evening transmission period. This figure was almost as high among the 'veterans' – those who had had sets since the service was revived in 1946 – as among recent recruits. And this despite the fact that the viewer had no choice of programmes. A further 4 per cent of the Television sample (including 8 per cent of the veterans) would be resisting the lure of viewing and be listening to the radio but 19 per cent of the Control group would be listening; so on the assumption that the Control group's behaviour represented 'normality', it could be said that, at times when viewing was possible, the presence of the television set reduced listening by nearly four-fifths.

The inquiries showed a significant increase in viewing with each step down the educational scale. Viewers who switched on their sets at 8.00 p.m. were likely to be hooked for the rest of the evening. There seemed to be little discrimination in viewing and this meant that many viewers must be watching programmes of kinds which they would have actively avoided on radio. This had obvious social implications to which we called the BBC's attention but it also had technical implications for Audience Research of which more will be said later.

The quantification of the way leisure time was spent before and after television invaded homes, which emerged from this and subsequent studies both here and in other countries, ultimately led to a better understanding of the dynamics of television's effects on other leisure activities. Some years later Professor Wilbur Schramm was to sum the situation up when writing of the way television affected children's leisure patterns, though in my view what he said applied in almost equal measure to adults. He wrote that 'when TV comes in *functionally similar* activities will be replaced, whereas functionally different ones will not; that certain activities (for example, radio listening) will be *transformed* in function and that *marginal* or *unorganised* activities will be replaced before purposive and organised ones.'

The function which an activity performs is, of course, subjectively defined. The primary function of the nightly visit to the local may for one man be social and for another the need to quench thirst. One man may garden primarily for exercise and another primarily for the prestige of producing the prize-winning vegetable marrow. Viewing television performs different functions for different people – and for the same person at different times. One child may be glued to the screen because of the need to satisfy an appetite for vicarious excitement; another because he knows he cannot keep his end up when he plays with his peer-group.

But it is probably fair to say that, for most people most of the time that they view, the function of television is to provide a convenient and easily accessible pastime – in the literal sense of the word. Viewing feels, even though it is not in fact, 'for free'. It is anything but physically strenuous. It offers scope for fantasy, for those who want fantasy, and scope for 'keeping in touch' and the proverbial widening of the horizons for those who want their horizons widened.

Much the same could be said of the radio listening which at one time occupied a high proportion of the evening leisure hours – but not of the radio listening which performed the function of relieving the boredom of housework, of washing the baby or the car or the function of relieving the nagging ache of loneliness. So it is not surprising that radio's evening audiences have dwindled away while its day-time audiences have been largely unaffected.

Similarly the habit of family cinema-going, which was primarily for the entertainment which it offered, had a function similar to that of viewing and, as every circuit knows, has shrunk severely since television's advent; but significantly adolescent cinema-going, the function of which was to provide an escape from the family if not an opportunity for necking in a dark warm environment, has been much more resistant to the inroads of viewing.

Physical activities like playing out-door games, many social activities and almost certainly all creative hobbies which really grip their participants serve functions which contrast with those served by viewing. All the evidence suggests that the attractions of viewing television are not strong enough seriously to reduce participation in such activities as these, whereas it does make considerable inroads into what Schramm describes as 'marginal' and 'unorganised' ways of spending leisure but which schoolboys graphically, if less scientifically, describe as 'just messing about' and which occupy more of the time of most of us than we care to admit.

We were ready to launch continuous audience research for television in December 1949 and this involved my first experience of appearing on the screen. I had to broadcast an appeal for viewers' co-operation, explaining what we were after, why I thought it worth doing and what their co-operation would involve. I had broadcast on radio a number of times before but this, I found, was very different. There could be no relying on reading a carefully prepared script – one had to memorise what one wanted to say. But speaking to camera was in one way more natural than speaking into a microphone. In a radio studio one was alone in what felt like a gold-fish bowl, the nearest humans being the engineer and the producer the other side of a sound-proof pane of glass. Although being televised meant sitting alone in a dazzling pool of light in a studio which seemed as vast as one of the larger railway termini, one could at least address oneself to the cameraman even though, in common with every one else in the studio, he was in total darkness.

The response to the appeal was staggering. Offers of help came from over 24,000 viewing families – one in eight of all those who then had television sets. This was, I am sure, less a measure of any eloquence of mine than of the degree of interest and involvement in television which still characterised the viewing public.

Our plan was to set up a Viewing Panel with a changing membership of 600, each being asked to serve for three months. Like members of the Listening Panels they would be asked to answer questions about those programmes which they happened to hear, or rather see. But the first need was to discover how far those who had responded were representative of the viewing public as a whole. Each of the 24,000 was therefore sent a questionnaire asking for information which would enable us to compare them with the viewing public as we had found it to be when we had studied it, by stringent statistical methods, in the 1948 inquiry. We also asked them to tell us about their tastes in television programmes and to say whether they would be willing, if called upon to do so, to take part in further research.

Nearly 19,400 questionnaires were returned completed and their distribution corresponded very closely to that of the viewing public in terms of the length of time they had had their sets, the kinds of sets they had and their radio reception facilities. In terms of the Income of the Head of the Household, the respondents to the appeal were a bit short of the most-, and the least, well-off as these figures show (the income categories, appropriate only twenty-five years ago, seem incredible today):

Annual Income of Head of Household (in £)	Appeal Respondents %	1948 Sample %
Over 1000	17	21
650 – 1000	23	26
350 – 650	46	35
Less than 350	14	18
	100	100

The number of adults (over 16-year-olds) per household was 2.60 in both groups, but the number of children in the respondent families averaged 0.82, whereas in the 1948 sample it was 0.52. (We wondered whether this discrepancy might have been due to the way we had asked the question: we had invited the respondents to tell us 'the number of people in their household', maybe some of them had included the children who might just as well be considered as 'in their household' in view of the time they came in from next door in order to watch television!) All things considered we were satisfied that the response had come from what could be regarded as a pretty fair cross-section of the viewing public and since all but 800 of the respondents had said they were willing to give further help this would also apply to those upon whom we should have to depend for the recruitment of our panel.

Tastes in television output were ascertained by inviting each member of the responding families to record his/her attitude to each of eighteen categories of programme. They could say they 'liked it very much', 'liked it moderately', 'didn't like it much', 'strongly disliked it' or were neutral, perhaps because they hadn't seen any. This is what emerged:

	Like Very Much %	Like Moderately %	Neutral %	Don't Much Like %	Strongly Dislike %
PLAYS					
in the Studio	83	11	5	1	—
in Theatres	28	45	13	12	2
LIGHT ENTERTAINMENT					
Music Hall type	34	36	5	12	13
Revue	28	39	11	16	6
Musical Comedy	33	35	12	16	4
Cabaret	60	27	4	7	2
MUSIC					
Ballet and solo singing	25	24	6	27	18
Opera	16	22	17	25	20
Instrumental recitals	20	30	9	25	16
OUTSIDE BROADCASTS					
Sports	51	25	7	13	4
Public & ceremonial events	55	30	5	8	2
Other o.bs.	43	37	17	3	—
STUDIO TALKS AND DEMONSTRATIONS	32	36	10	17	5
FILMS					
Newsreels	84	14	1	1	—
Documentaries	40	37	9	12	2
Feature films	41	31	6	14	8
MAGAZINE PROGRAMMES	49	34	5	9	3
FOR THE CHILDREN	41	26	26	5	2

We analysed the answers in terms of the (head of household) income, sex, age and the length of time the viewer had had his/her set. We found that with each step *up* the income scale there was a sharply diminishing taste for all types of Light

Entertainment and for Feature films and decreasing taste for Ballet and for Documentary films. The tastes of men and women proved very much alike except that women showed more interest than men in Musical Comedy, Ballet and Magazine programmes while more than twice as high a proportion of men (70 per cent) as of women (33 per cent) expressed enthusiasm for Outside Broadcasts of Sport.

The age analysis distinguished between children of 7–11 and 12–14, the older groupings being 15–19, 20–24, 25–49, 50–59 and 60 & over. *For the Children* was 'liked very much' by 89 per cent of the 7–11-year-olds and 52 per cent of the 12–14s but also by substantial minorities of the older groups. A startling two thirds of 7–11-year-olds claimed to like Cabaret 'very much' but that they were not indiscriminatingly expressing enthusiasm for everything was shown by the small proportions of them who said the same of such categories as Opera, Instrumental Recitals, Studio Plays or Plays from the theatre. The 12s–14s stood out as the group with the highest proportion of enthusiasts for Cabaret, O.Bs. of Sport, Newsreels and Feature films.

The next two age groups, 15–19 and 20–24, were noticeably less free with expressions of enthusiasm than either younger or older viewers, but more of them than of any older group said they liked Ballet and Feature films 'very much' for both of which enthusiasm steadily diminished with age. Studio Plays claimed pre-eminence in every adult age-group and Newsreels in every group including children.

There was nothing in the analysis in terms of 'age of set' to suggest that, as the television public expanded, its tastes would change, though the most recent viewers, understandably, tended to be the most ecstatic.

The questions about programme tastes had been included for two reasons. We knew that viewers would enjoy answering them so that their inclusion would encourage the completion of the questionnaire as a whole. But more importantly we were interested in comparing the tastes of those willing and unwilling to participate in further research. To this end, too, we had included a question about general interest in television. Their respective attitudes towards different categories of programme were substantially similar but, as we expected, the 'unwilling' were distinctly less enthusiastic about television than were the 'willing', as these figures show:

	Extremely Interested %	Very Interested %	Moderately Interested %	Not Particularly Interested %	Not at all Interested %
Willing	53	36	11	—	—
Unwilling	43	44	13	—	—

The questionnaire also asked the viewer to say approximately how many evenings a week his set was switched on Here are the answers:

	Number of evenings of viewing per week				Average
	1–4 %	5 %	6 %	7 %	
Willing	8	20	57	15	5·78
Unwilling	14	22	43	21	5·66

That the Unwilling should view rather less than the Willing was, of course, consistent with their being rather less enthusiastic about television, but the difference was small and certainly not large enough to cause us misgivings at the thought that we should have to rely on the Willing to staff our panels and so to represent the feelings of the television public as a whole about the programmes they saw. Incidentally the finding that two-thirds of the television public viewed six, if not seven, nights a week vividly confirmed the findings of the 1948 inquiry that the appetite for television was pretty substantial.

When the Viewing Panel got under way, in January 1950, the Willing proved as good as their word; virtually all those who were asked to man the first drafts agreed to do so and even a year later we could still be sure of more than 90 per cent of our invitations being accepted. Furthermore, their level of performance was excellent; during the first year the average rate of return of the weekly packages of questionnaires was 88 per cent.

The device we had developed for arriving at a numerical measure of the audience's overall attitude to particular radio programmes was also employed for television programmes. Each Listening Panel member, it will be recalled, was required to 'sum up his reactions' to each programme he heard by selecting from a five-point scale which ran the gamut of possible emotions from ecstacy to despair. From their use of this scale an Appreciation Index was calculated. However, in the light of our discovery that, in those single service days, viewers were much less discriminating than listeners, direct comparison of Appreciation Indices for television with those for radio programmes might well lead to wrong conclusions. To discourage this, we decided to give them distinctive names: we continued to issue Appreciation Indices for radio programmes but those for television programmes were to be known as Reaction Indices.

The case of Christopher Fry's verse drama *The Lady's Not For Burning* was a startling illustration of the difference between the attitudes of viewers and listeners in those days. When broadcast in the Third Programme, this play had been enthusiastically received by its audience but when, later, it was televised its viewing audience gave it the bird. There was no reason to think that the television production was to blame; like that of the radio production it was acclaimed by the critics as exemplary. The explanation almost certainly lay in differences between the two audiences. Those who had heard it on the Third undoubtedly included many who were already familiar with the play or, if they were not, knew from experience what to expect there; it would be no shock to them to be faced with an unconventional form. But the audience of viewers was very different. Not only was it many times larger, but it was far less sophisticated. The vast majority of them would have said that when they viewed they 'expected to be entertained' and Fry's play, so unlike anything they had ever experienced before, was certainly not what *they* called 'entertainment'.

During the first two years of the Viewing Panel's existence its members were asked to do more than record their feelings about the programmes which they saw. Each was provided with a list of the forthcoming week's programmes and asked to 'log' the number of people (if any) who had viewed each one. We used these data to provide us with information about the quantity of viewing that had taken place. This was a temporary expedient, to last only until there were enough viewers for it to be practicable for television audiences to be measured with our daily samples of the population as a whole. We knew that we could not project these data to give us the actual numbers of the audiences for, since the Panel viewed more than the generality of the television public, this would have lead to exaggerated estimates. But we were reasonably satisfied that, as between one programme and another, they would not give us a seriously distorted picture, so it was a situation which could be endured with equanimity for the time being. And it was interesting while it lasted, for since it told us how many of the Panel's sets were tuned in to each programme and also how many people were viewing it, we were able to observe the variations in the number of persons viewing *per set-in-use* (of which more will be said in a later chapter). The mean size of the groups gathered round sets-in-use proved to be 2.47 – the average size of the Panel family being 3.42. (For more than half the evening programmes over 70 per cent of the Panel's sets were switched on and for only one programme in four were there less than 40 per cent.)

At the end of 1951 our daily interview Survey was able to take over; from then on it was to be known as the Survey of Listening *and Viewing.* In October-December 1952 the Survey's samples were showing that the Television Public consisted of 14 per cent of the population and that these people were viewing for an average of one hour and three minutes each evening, i.e. for just over 40 per cent of the time that television programmes were on the air.

By October-December 1953 the Television Public had grown to 22 per cent of the population and evening viewing averaged one hour six minutes per head. A year later (the last October-December of the monopoly era), the Television Public was 31 per cent and evening viewing had increased to one hour twenty-three minutes per head, but as by this time programme hours had been extended (by a 7.00 p.m. instead of a 7.30 start), the Television Public was still viewing for much the same *proportion* of available programme time.

For broadcasting, the most notable event in these years was undoubtedly the Coronation on 13th June, 1953. At least some part of the Coronation Service in Westminster Abbey was either seen on television or heard on the radio by 88 per cent of the adult population of the United Kingdom. The BBC had never before had so large a domestic audience. The listening audience accounted for 37 per cent and nearly all of them had heard it in their own homes. The viewing audience was 51 per cent, but more than half of them saw the Service in the homes of friends or in public places such as shops, cinemas or pubs.

The mushrooming of television was intoxicating for those who were professionally engaged in it, but those who thought about the society they lived in began to express concern about its consequences. There were inevitably some extravagant prognostications: some said that universal television would prove to be the new opium of the people; others said it would raise the general cultural level to hitherto undreamed of heights; there were confident predictions that it would destroy family life/reinstate the centrality of the home, create a race of supine spectators/stimulate participation in new interests, crush/revive individuality and so on. Although the more exuberant prophets of doom or the new dawn were not to be taken very seriously – parallel prophecies had greeted previous innovations from the invention of printing to the introduction of compulsory education – there was a case to answer. If every home would soon have its television set and viewing become the principal way in which leisure would be spent, this could not fail to have *some* social consequences. It was inevitable and proper that their nature should be a matter for speculation – and study.

Many of even the more thoughtful speculations seemed to take it for granted that these consequences would depend solely upon what was transmitted, as though the viewer's role was wholly passive – that of a clean slate, waiting to be written on. (It may be said in passing that if this were so, then television's impact would be relatively easy to regulate – all that would be necessary would be the exercise of effective control over what was transmitted – and the study of television's impact would call for no more than a careful analysis of its content.)

The reality is, of course, quite different. The viewer is not a mere passive recipient, he is an active participant. Viewing is an encounter between the seen and the seer. The seer brings to this encounter his predispositions and his prejudices, his tastes and his opinions – indeed the whole body of his experience. This is why the same stimulus – the programme – notoriously evokes totally different reactions from different viewers and even from the same viewer at different times. (If the phrase 'The Impact of Television' carries overtones of an active agent bearing upon an inert mass, it is infelicitous. The matter of concern would be more aptly described as 'The Effects of Viewing': 'The Effects' rather than 'The Impact', 'of Viewing' rather than 'of Television'.)

A failure to take adequate account of the part played by the viewer inevitably results in extravagant forecasts of the extent to which viewing can change viewers. This is because most viewers, most of the time, don't want to be changed – and take steps to see that they are not – and indirectly because virtually all viewers acquire television sets in order to be entertained (though they may differ widely about what constitutes entertainment).

It is, perhaps, just as well for the cohesion and stability of society that people don't lightly change their established tastes or values, opinions or habits of behaviour, whether these be conventional or non-conformist. They tend to feel that the devil they do know is to be preferred to the devil they don't. Moreover, they know from experience that while the process of changing may be exciting and stimulating, it may also be uncomfortable, if not painful. It follows that any attempt to effect a change from outside comes up against powerful conservative forces to which, no doubt, inertia and laziness as well as healthy scepticism contribute. That viewing is primarily a relaxation reinforces the viewer's resistance to change, for change necessarily calls for effort, but effort and relaxation are not natural bed-fellows.

To be sure, the skills of television producers may be deployed to overcome the viewer's resistance to being changed, but it should not be forgotten that the viewer has a well-tested system of defences. In the first place he can refrain from switching on any programme which he doesn't want to see and, if he does switch it on, he is free to switch it off at any moment he chooses. If the compulsiveness of television inhibits him from doing either he can, if he is bored, easily lower the level of his attention so that he is literally 'taking no notice'. Failing that, he can fall back on the weapon of selective perception which can go a long way towards ensuring that what he *does* 'take in' is congenial even if, to make it so, he has had unconsciously to distort it. Finally, if all else fails, he can quickly forget what he has seen, which he is quite likely to do if his interest had not been engaged (and which is made all the easier by the relentless succession of programmes).

Viewers are thus far from being defenceless victims of the propagandists or fruits ripe for the evangelists' picking. It is not surprising that the unanimous findings of research have been that television, in common with the other mass media, is far more effective in reinforcing existing tastes, values, opinions, attitudes and habits than in changing them. This is not to deny that television is a powerful agent for the exercise of the arts of gentle persuasion (to put it no higher, the success of television advertising is proof enough of that). But this is a proposition which needs no bush. The foregoing arguments have been deployed only because they are so often overlooked and, as a consequence, television's powers of persuasion overstated.

The BBC fully shared the public concern about the effects of viewing and was anxious that it should be properly studied. The problem was remitted to Audience Research and we discussed it with our Advisory Committee of Psychologists early in the fifties. The upshot was a decision to split the problem into two: the effects on children and its effects on adults. Public concern about the former was a good deal greater and consisted principally of misgivings in face of the evident enthusiasm of children for television and the scarifying accounts of child-addiction which were reaching this country from the U.S.A.

It was felt that the study of the effects of viewing on children would be so formidable an undertaking that a distinct full-time research team would have to be set up to tackle it and that the problem was so contentious that there would be considerable advantages if the work was done under wholly independent auspicies.' To cut a long story short, I was deputed to approach Farrar Brown, the then Director of the Nuffield Foundation. One meeting with him in the Foundation's elegant home in Regent's Park was sufficient to enlist his support for an approach with specific proposals to the Trustees. Under the benign chairmanship of Sir Hector Hetherington, they agreed to sponsor and finance a study, to be directed by Dr (later Professor) Hilde Himmelweit of the LSE. She gathered a team about her whose principal other members were Bram Oppenheim and Pamela Vince and they set to work. Her report, *Television and the Child*, which proved a classic in its field, was published in 1958.

The main source of the Nuffield inquiry's evidence was a survey carried out in London, Portsmouth, Sunderland and Bristol in which 4,500 children were tested. Two age groups, 10–11 and 13–14, were studied, each child from a television home being matched with a similar child from a home which had not yet a TV set (and there were still plenty of these). There was also a 'before-and-after' study in Norwich which had only just been reached by television. Children were tested before the Norwich transmitter opened and again a year later. A number of smaller supplementary studies were carried out, amongst mothers and teachers for example, of children's understanding and recall of specific programmes, of the effects of viewing on school performance and of the content of television programmes.

The findings, as was expected, showed that children were very heavy viewers. 'The amount a child views', the report said, 'depends in the first instance on his intelligence, secondly on his personality and on how full and active a life he had led before television came on the scene, and thirdly on parental example.' One finding, which was to make a considerable impression on the report's readers, was the extent to which children viewed 'adult' programmes between 6.00 and 9.00 p.m.

There was nothing very surprising in the finding that a

child's preferences were 'a function of his sex, emotional and intellectual maturity and his own idiosyncratic needs'. The report noted that the chance of a child's viewing programmes falling outside his normal preferences, but which he might have come to enjoy, was diminished by the availability of alternative services: if he could find what he wanted by switching from channel to channel, he did so.

Television's appeal for children lay partly in its easy availability as a time-filler. It offered the satisfaction of being in the know; to some it offered the security and reassurance of the familiar, to others the excitement of suspense and constant change. The inquiry found no convincing evidence that viewing aggressive programmes *caused* aggressive behaviour in children, but they also found no evidence that such programmes were positively beneficial. Viewing did not do much to improve children's general knowledge, but it did not seem to affect their school performance nor their interest in school or school societies. Reading skills were also largely unaffected, but the enquiry did note that viewing stimulated interest in reading through its serial dramatisations. Teachers frequently alleged that viewing made children more passive. The inquiry found no evidence to support this. At the same time there was also little evidence that viewing made children more enterprising or stimulated new interests for them.

So brief a summary does far less than justice to the Nuffield Report which did not confine itself to the presentation of evidence but went on to the induction of principles of both theoretical importance and practical application. Its publication was taken very seriously. The Director-General of the BBC set up an internal study group to examine its findings and report to him. Later the BBC and the ITA jointly appointed a committee of outside persons of eminence to look into its implications and their report was published (*Children and Television Programmes*, BBC & ITV 1960). This was followed by a generous grant by the ITA for further research and, through a chain of circumstances which need not be spelt out here, this ultimately lead to the setting up of the Centre for Mass Communications Research at Leicester University. Although it would be difficult to point to specific changes in policy as directly attributable to the Nuffield Report, there is no doubt that its influence, and that of the later American study, entitled *Television in the lives of our Children* (Schramm, Lyle & Parker, Stanford University Press, 1961) were pervasive; they conditioned the thinking of a generation of planners and producers of programmes for children.

The Stanford report appeared three years after the Nuffield. Though it dealt with American and Canadian children and with transatlantic television, there was a considerable correspondence in the findings of the two. The flavours of Schramm's book can be judged from these quotations from it:

'... the child is introduced to the mass media almost wholly as fantasy ... in the child's most pliable and impressionable years. The way he begins to use television is *for fantasy* and this is so deeply ingrained in a child that he often has the greatest difficulty in thinking of *educational* television, let us say, as a proper use of the medium.'

'Young children, as we know, give themselves wholly to television. They are critical, not of the art, but of what the characters do or of what is done to them.'

'The more a child has a "parent problem", the more he tends to seek his satisfactions and work out his aggressions with fantasy, to select the audiovisual entertainment media rather than the printed ones.'

'It is unlikely that the level of gratification children can obtain from television will ever be as high as they can obtain from life. Television is in large measure a substitute activity.'

'The thing that impresses us is how deeply engrained in a child the love of activity is.... The vicarious satisfactions a child can get through television are almost invariably lower on his heirarchy than the satisfactions he can get directly – providing, of course, he *can* get the direct ones.'

'... we see no evidence whatsoever that television *makes* a child withdrawn, or *makes* passivity. Rather, it encourages and reinforces those tendencies *when they exist in dangerous amounts*.'

'It was not this violence (fighting, gun-play, etc.) that seemed chiefly to frighten the children whom we had watching these programmes. Rather it was the dark and mysterious scenes – for example, a picture that was mostly in the dark, and a scene in which persons dug for a body in a cellar – or the scenes into which they could easily put themselves, such as a person uncovering tarantulas by turning over a rock.'

'The roots of delinquency ... grow from the home life, the neighbourhood life, and the disturbed personality. The most that television can do is to feed the malignant impulses that already exist.'

At the time when it was decided to seek outside sponsorship for the study of the effects of viewing upon children, there was no alternative but to leave that of its effects on adults to the Audience Research Department, for there was then no academic group or Institute capable of, or interested in, taking this under its wing. While we welcomed this assignment we knew that anything we did would be bound to be limited in scope and protracted. It would only be one of a number of jobs P. & D. had to do and, since it was not directly concerned with current programmes, could not be given priority. In the event it proved something of an Old Man of the Sea for it was not until 1960 that we were able to produce a report upon it.

The first thing we did was to consider the kinds of effect viewing might have and invite the Advisory Group of Psychologists to select the fields upon which they thought our study should concentrate. Their choice fell on Family Life and in particular on the extent to which, if at all, the possession of a TV set focused on a family's interest in its home and had a unifying influence on the family.

The inquiry was given to Belson to tackle under the supervision of a committee consisting of Professor Rex Knight (Chairman), Lady Wootton, and Professors Philip Vernon and Maurice Kendall. It was decided to place the main weight on measuring changes in relevant behaviour which accompanied the acquisition of television, in particular in the incidence of 'home-centred' activities, in the level and diversity of sociable activities, and in 'visiting' either by, or of, viewers.

It cannot be claimed that the findings were spectacular. The possession of a TV set *did* keep families at home, but the extent to which it did so was modest simply because most viewers had spent most of their leisure at home even before they bought their sets. (This did not contradict the evidence that some activities, such as cinema-going, were severely reduced, for a reduction of out-of-home activities could be simultaneously 'small' and 'large'; 'small' if it were expressed as a proportion of all families and 'large' if it were expressed as a proportion of those who previously spent their leisure away from home.)

The incidence amongst viewers of home-centred activities, joint-activities with other members of the family and sociable activities in general could not be said to be strikingly different from that amongst comparable non-viewers, so if these were fair measure of *attitudes* towards home, it could not be said that television was affecting them very much. The acquisition of a TV set was accompanied, it is true, by considerable changes in the incidence of visiting, but all the indications were that this was temporary and would disappear once every family had its own set. My own feeling was that the inquiry had demonstrated the resilience of family life, its capacity to resist change and its ability, when faced with a potentially disturbing intruder, to absorb and digest it.

But although this inquiry did not produce sensational findings, it was far from unimportant methodologically for Belson developed novel ways both of defining and of measuring forms of behaviour and of 'matching' subjects and controls. This matching procedure, which he called the Stable Correlate method, is fully documented in his *The Impact of Television* (Crosby Lockwood, 1967) which also reports the further work he did in this field after he left us to become Head of the Survey Research Centre at the LSE.

With the issue of the Knight Committee's report, *Television and the Family* in 1960, our work in the field of the social – as distinct from the broadcasting-centred – effects of viewing was for the time thankfully left on one side, indeed by the time it came again to the fore I had retired as Head of Audience Research.

11 Enter ITV

Once the Television Act of 1953 left no further doubt that commercial (to be known, rather oddly, as independent) television was to be permitted we had to decide what kind of ITV audience information the BBC would need and how we could provide it. The most obvious need would be for measurements of ITV's audiences in terms which would make possible direct comparisons with similar information about BBC output. There could be no question about what should be done: we would have to widen the scope of our Survey of Listening and Viewing by requiring our interviewers to ask people about their viewing of ITV programmes in just the same way they asked about viewing of BBC-TV and listening to BBC Radio programmes. Plans were therefore made for this to begin from the first moment the ITV went on the air on 22nd September, 1955.

As it was equally obvious that the Programme Contractors, advertisers and advertising agents would all need similar information about the consumption of ITV programmes, it seemed crazy for the work, which would be expensive, to be done more than once. I therefore suggested to the BBC Management that we should offer to make our audience measurement findings available to 'the other side' for a fee which should at least recompense us for the extra expense in which the measurement of ITV viewing would involve us. The suggestion was accepted.

The advertising agents and advertisers had set up an *ad hoc* committee to consider and recommend what should be done to meet their needs for audience measurement. It so happened that its Chairman was George Harrison, of the London Press Exchange, under whom I had served twenty years earlier. I like to think that this helped to bring the negotiations to a quick

Enter ITV   175

and successful conclusion when Sir Ian Jacob, then D-G and I went to see him.

The agreement was for one year in the first instance; after that it lapsed. There was no suggestion that our service had fallen short – indeed a number of agents privately assured me that they would have been happy for it to have continued especially as, by the standards of the world of advertising, its cost was trifling. The objections came from the larger advertisers who demanded a system of measurement which would provide data about the precise moments at which their commercials were being shown. Only a meter system could do that so they insisted on having a meter system – regardless of its cost, which was prodigious.

In the months running up to ITV's opening day two companies offering meter services had joined battle. Television Audience Measurement (TAM) – an offshoot of a well-known advertising agency – was fighting it out with the A. C. Neilson Co. Inc. of Chicago which had already swept the board in the U.S.A. with the Neilson Rating Service. Both were determined to provide a service from ITV's outset, to individual subscribers if necessary though each hoped to land a contract with a consortium embracing all interested parties including, they hoped, the BBC.

During visits to the States I had many times been assured with bated breath that whatever you thought about Art Neilson you had to hand it to him as a Salesman so when I was invited to a luncheon at which the Great Man himself would give a Presentation, I looked forward to it with curiosity. Neilson had set up his H.Q. in a suite of appropriate magnificence at the Dorchester. After a somewhat ponderously convivial lunch we were ushered into an adjoining room for the presentation.

Neilson's case was essentially simple and could have been effectively deployed in at most twenty minutes. It lasted fifty, though it seemed longer. Its protraction was achieved by the use of what I suppose would now be called a teaching-aid. By his side was a set of display cards on an easel. Each card bore one or two words – very occasionally three – presumably intended to drive home the Message. If my memory serves me, one bore the word, say, EFFICIENT, another SWIFT, another ECONOMICAL and another MOMENT-BY-MOMENT. A deferential aide stood by to whisk away each card as Neilson's elephantine exposition disposed of its point. When we finally emerged, blinking, into the sunlight of Park Lane, I overheard one of my fellow-guests muttering grimly that after this experience of paralysing boredom not even the Archangel Gabriel would induce him to subscribe to this service.

In due course a joint industry contract was negotiated and no one was surprised that it went to TAM. Neilson bravely carried on his operation for a time but soon an 'amalgamation' was announced which, to the outsider, looked much more like TAM's absorption of Neilson's TV-rating service. (When the contract came up for review, some years later, TAM lost it to a firm which, ironically, had been set up by a group of ex-TAM Directors who had been summarily ejected by its Chairman after an internal row. Their service is now referred to as JICTAR, standing for the Joint Industry Committee for Television Advertising Research, the commissioning body.)

TAM was keen that the BBC should subscribe to its service for this would certainly have added to its prestige, but for several reasons we decided not to do so. It was not that we thought that there was anything unsound about TAM's specifications, or that TAM would not be able to meet them, but rather that these specifications did not meet our needs. TAM was to confine its attention to viewing families able to receive both ITV and BBC programmes. At first these would be only a tiny minority of Britain's television families and though their numbers would surely increase, it was likely to be some years before all viewers came into this category. We, of course, were interested in all the viewing of BBC programmes; in that which took place in 'single-channel', as much as 'multi-channel' homes (and, for that matter, also in viewing in public places or in the homes of neighbours). This meant that if we had subscribed to TAM we would still have had to maintain our own system to complete the picture. We should thus have saved little or nothing to off-set the cost of the subscription – and that would, by BBC standards, have been prodigious, for a meter-system was inevitably very costly to run. Furthermore – and this was cogent even after the number of 'single-channel' homes had dwindled to insignificance – we felt it to be important to employ the same methods of measurement to viewing as to listening so that we could supply a comprehensive picture of the consumption of broadcasting as a whole. But the measurement of listening was not within TAM's terms of reference.

Our decision to go it alone was not taken without a full realisation of the consequences. The simultaneous operation of two radically different systems of audience measurement was bound to lead to trouble – and certainly did. (Two similar systems based on sampling might well produce differing findings not because either was 'wrong' but because of the operation of chance. This was dramatically demonstrated when TAM and Neilson both advertised their services by publishing their results for the first day of one of the ITV stations only to reveal that their respective findings did not coincide.)

The principal, but not the only, bone of contention concerned the way in which the BBC and ITV 'shared the audience'. This would have been 'news' in any case for ITV had been brought into being expressly to 'provide an alternative' to the BBC, but when it was realised that the two contenders were disagreeing about how the audience was being shared, the news story gained considerable spice.

We expressed our estimates of the way the audience was being shared in terms of percentages which came to be known as the BBC:ITV ratio. The very first ratio we published, which was for October 1955, the first month of competition, was BBC 57:ITV 43. Spelt out, this meant that we estimated that those who had facilities for viewing ITV as well as BBC programmes had devoted to BBC programmes 57 per cent, and to ITV programmes 43 per cent, of the time they spent in viewing. But TAM also published estimates of the BBC:ITV ratio and it soon became apparent that not only did this differ from ours but that TAM invariably showed the ITV's share of the audience to be greater, and the BBC's to be correspondingly less, than we showed them to be.

M

Many of my colleagues were indignant about this. They had come to place their faith in the veracity of BBC Audience Research and couldn't believe that TAM's estimates were to be trusted. Some went so far as to assert that if 'the other side' were not actually cooking the books, they must have deliberately chosen a method of measurement which was calculated to show ITV to an advantage. I did my utmost to counter such views – risking the charge that 'all you research chaps stick together'. I argued that even the most cynical would have to admit that TAM would be stupid to falsify its findings for its livelihood depended on its professional respectability. As to the choice of the meter-method, there was hard evidence that this was a case of those who were paying the piper getting what they wanted to know – what happened at the precise moments that commercials were being shown. In any case any effect the choice of method might have on the way the BBC and ITV shared the audience couldn't have been foreseen when the choice was made, nor would advertisers have been much concerned whatever this effect were (Programme Contractors were another matter, but they hadn't had the decisive voice in the choice). No doubt some of the supporters of commercial television were equally ready to believe that the BBC did not use the meter-method because it might show the BBC to a disadvantage. But this was equally unfounded. We had made our decision, as has been shown, on quite different grounds.

To dismiss these as the causes of the discrepancies did not, however, do anything to explain them. The bewildered layman wanted to know which estimates, TAM's or ours, was 'right', or indeed if either were to be believed, though it would have been more sensible to have asked which was nearer to the truth. Naturally no one was more anxious to solve this problem than the researchers on both sides, but it wasn't an easy problem to solve, not the least because it was likely that the discrepancies were the product of several interacting causes.

When we and TAM talked about 'sharing the audience' did we mean the same thing by the 'audience'? Were the methods used by TAM, or those we used, biased by their very nature and if so, in what direction and how seriously? These were the kind of questions which the issue raised and an invitation in

1966 to deliver a BBC Lunchtime Lecture on a subject of my own choosing gave me a chance to explore them at some length. I called it *The Measurement of Audiences* and made the point that, paradoxically, the word audience had no generally accepted meaning in the context of broadcasting. I said:

'Having taken over the word from the theatre, cinema, or concert hall, where it has a generally agreed meaning, we have overlooked the fact that it cannot be applied to broadcasting in a similarly precise way. The audience for a performance of a play is the people who were present in the theatre when it was performed. They are in a sense a "captive" audience. But the people who are exposed to a broadcast are not similarly captive. Some of them, it is true, may remain in their chairs throughout, enthralled from start to finish by what they hear or see; some, though present in the room, may virtually ignore the broadcast their set is receiving, and some may be present for only part of the time. Is the listener who reads a newspaper to the accompaniment of a radio discussion part of its audience or is he not? Can a viewer who is called several times to the telephone in the course of watching a play be regarded as having seen it? If mother tolerates *Sportsview* only because father wants it on, is she part of the audience?

'The answers to such questions as these depend, of course, on how you choose to define the term "audience". You may choose to define it conservatively, confining it to those who have given the broadcast their full attention throughout, or you can define it generously, including all within earshot, or indeed you can choose any point along this continuum. But whatever your decision, be assured that it is highly relevant to the question of audience size, for if a broadcast's audience is deemed to include all within earshot it may be many times larger than if it is deemed to exclude all but the fully attentive.

'What is deemed to be "viewing" in practice varies from one system of audience measurement to another. This is inevitable, if only because what it is possible to measure varies from one system to another. There is no harm and indeed there may be positive advantages in this so long as people do not expect the audience estimates produced by different systems to agree. The moment they start looking over one another's shoulders the trouble begins. One system will be found to have estimated the audience for a certain broadcast to be *x*, whereas another stimates it to be *y*, and the layman, naturally enough, throws up his hands in despair. But if they are using the word "audience" in different senses maybe their answers ought to differ because they are not measuring the same thing.'

There was one glaring difference between what we and TAM respectively meant by the word 'audience'. For us it meant people and for TAM it meant TV-sets. Our method was based on questioning samples of the population about their previous day's viewing; TAM's was based on metered records of when the TV-sets in a sample of homes had been switched on and the stations to which they had been tuned. (It soon became habitual for people to refer to 'families-viewing' when what was really meant was 'sets-in-use'. Our method provided no information about the number of sets which had been switched on to a programme just as TAM's meters could provide no information about the number of people who had viewed it.

(Incidentally this meant that, in practice, our BBC:ITV ratios, or indeed any comparison we made of two competing programmes, were almost certain to differ from TAM's because the number of viewers per set-in-use was liable to vary from programme to programme. A hypothetical, but plausible, case can illustrate this. Suppose that one million sets were switched on to Programme *A* and two million to Programme *B*, its competitor. Suppose further that the average number of viewers per-set-switched-on to *A* were 1.5 and to *B* were 3.0 so that *A* had one and a half million viewers and *B* had six million. The comparison would then look like this:

Programme	Number of sets-in-use	%
A	1,000,000	33
B	2,000,000	67
	3,000,000	100

Programme	Number of viewers	%
A	1,500,000	20
B	6,000,000	80
	7,500,000	100

If the 'audience' being 'shared' were sets-in-use, then *A* could claim one-third; but if it were viewers then *A's* share would only be one-fifth.)

Had the methods we used any built-in biases in favour of BBC-TV or TAM's any bias in favour of ITV? (A built-in bias is one which is inherent in the very nature of the method and not, of course, deliberately contrived.) Taking first the method we used I said:

'It has been suggested that because our interviewers, in introducing themselves to their informants and seeking their co-operation, say that they "come from the BBC", this may lead some informants to exaggerate the extent of their BBC viewing or to understate their viewing of ITV. We have carried out some experiments to test this but the results do not suggest that there is much substance in it. Another suggestion, which has recently been put to us by a friendly critic, is that the particular method of sampling we employ results in some under-representation of what in the world of market research is known as "the DE class". If this were so, then it would be likely to introduce some bias against ITV viewing because all the evidence indicates that it is in this stratum of the population that the ITV's share of the audience is greatest.'

I thought this would have some substance, but I very much doubted whether the magnitude of the bias which it introduced could have been more than marginal.

But TAM had its sampling problems too. Their samples consisted of families who had agreed to co-operate by allowing Tammeters to be installed in their homes and TAM engineers to call weekly to remove the recording tapes. As an inducement, TAM undertook to maintain the set in good order just as long as the Tammeter remained. But some of the families TAM needed for its samples wouldn't play (it was generally believed that the 'refusal rate' was about 15 per cent). As might be expected the refusal rate grew with each step up the social scale and the distortion of TAM's samples which this introduced tended to be detrimental to their estimates of the extent of viewing of BBC-TV because this also tended to increase with each step up the social scale. TAM, we knew, was well aware of this danger and did their utmost to correct it. If one Top Person refused to house a Tammeter they did not give up but went on until they found another who would. But the fact remained that in the final analysis TAM's samples inevitably consisted of people who would co-operate and left out all who wouldn't – and to that extent it was bound to be biased. But once again I am doubtful if such residual bias could have been serious.

In short, I hadn't much doubt that after every allowance had been made for the effects of bias there would still be discrepancies between our estimates and TAM's estimates of the way in which BBC-TV and ITV shared the audience and that it would be ours which would show the BBC to better advantage. But I went on to put forward a possible explanation. It was an extension of the argument that the discrepancies resulted from the differing meanings which we respectively attached to the word 'audience'.

I argued that if in fact it were true that ITV's share of the sets-in-use were greater than its share of the people who had been viewing, as it would be if both we and TAM were broadly correct, this could only mean that ITV programmes tended to be switched on and then ignored to a greater extent than those of BBC-TV. I said that:

'... direct statistical evidence on this point is unfortunately not available, but there is a strong *prima facie* case for believing that this is so. We know that there are some strong-minded viewers who only switch on the programmes they want to see and firmly switch them off when they end. But we also know that some sets are switched on as a matter of habit and then left on, tuned to the same channel, quite literally "regardless". Even if some of the time everyone in the room is viewing avidly, there will be other times when this or that member of the family loses interest and occupies himself or herself in other ways. He may not want the set off, for then he may "miss something", but at such times he is not a viewer – or not viewer enough to be recorded as such if questioned the following day.

'The pertinent point is that this kind of thing cannot be reflected in statistics based on sets-in-use. Every set which is switched on "counts" in this kind of enumeration, no matter how many or how few people are present, and no matter how many or how few are really viewing it. On the other hand, in statistics based on the methods we employ, an individual should not be counted as having viewed a broadcast unless he definitely recalled having done so; mere presence in the room where the set was switched on to it is not, by itself, enough.

'It follows from this that if one service tends to be switched on and left on, in the way described, to a greater extent than the other, then to that extent its "share" of the sets which are in use will be larger than its "share" of actual viewers.

'There is a great deal of evidence to suggest that, of the two services, it is ITV which is more often used in this way. This is hardly surprising, for few would deny that, at any rate in peak hours, the output of ITV, even though it is not consistently undemanding, certainly varies less in the level of its appeal than does the output of BBC television. (There is a limit to the frequency with which a commercially financed system of broadcasting can afford to alienate its regular customers.) It follows from this that those viewers who are disinclined to fiddle with the "channel knob" and who ask little of television at peak hours but successive programmes of undemanding entertainment which they can, if and when they feel so inclined, disregard are more likely to find satisfaction by settling for ITV than for BBC-TV.

'The conclusion to which this argument leads is that, other things being equal, ITV's share of the audience, when that means "share of the sets which are tuned in", will be greater than its share of the audience when that means "of people viewing". As the late C. E. M. Joad might have said, "It all depends on what you mean by audience".'

Before turning to other matters, one significant point should be noted: although we and TAM always differed in our estimates of the BBC:ITV ratio, these differences were strikingly consistent. Whenever the successive estimates of one of us showed a swing, the other's estimates would almost certainly show a similar swing, i.e. in the same direction and to about the same degree. In other words we tended to agree about *trends*. This was highly important because it was the trends in the ratios that mattered most to the policy-makers. For them, where they stood at any given time was less significant than where they were going. To be told that one method put the BBC's share at 48 per cent while the other put it at 52 per cent was not a matter of great moment (except to the P.R. men who knew the magic which sub-editors attached to the word 'majority'). But to be told that one method showed their share to be going up while the other showed it to be going down would have been very worrying. It was therefore reassuring that we and TAM seldom disagreed about the trends.

TAM's practice of issuing to the press weekly lists of the Top Twenty – the twenty broadcasts which their findings showed to have had the largest audiences – focused attention on the discrepancies between our findings and TAM's in respect of individual programmes (more exactly it focused attention within the BBC for, for reasons explained below, the Corporation did not publish its own Top Twenty). Whenever a comparison was made between TAM's Top Twenty and the one we might have issued, it was found that no more than seven or eight programmes appeared on both lists and that ITV programmes were virtually always in the lead in, and constituted the majority of, TAM's list. This was a constant source of irritation to those of my colleagues who took the trouble to make the comparison.

The reasons, whatever they were, for these discrepancies were, of course, the same as those for the discrepancies between the way the two services shared the audience since the latter were simply aggregation of findings about individual broadcasts. But these reason brought little comfort to those who saw ITV as, in their view, getting away with murder week after week. I was pressed to publish a weekly BBC Audience

Research Top Twenty as a counter-blast. The decision to publish was not mine to make, but I had some influence on the decision and always used it to oppose publication.

This had nothing to do with the fact that even our Top Twenty would mostly consist of ITV shows. Long before anyone had thought seriously of ending the BBC's monopoly I had opposed proposals that we should issue such lists for publicity purposes. My chief reason was a conviction that Top Twenties encouraged an entirely fallacious impression of the real significance of audience size: that every broadcast had the same target – the entire population – and that they were therefore all to be judged by the extent to which their audiences approached that goal. In fact, of course, each type of broadcast had its own target and these targets differed very widely. Popular light entertainment at a peak hour was indeed expected to attract a large audience but no one had similar expectations of, say, a late night concert of chamber music. There was no virtue in size *per se*, all that mattered was whether a broadcast attracted the audience which it was reasonable to expect of it. I felt very strongly that it would be wrong for the BBC to issue Top Twenties for this would make it even more difficult to dissuade people from the heretical belief that Bigger always meant Better.

Top Twenties were open to other objectives too. Some broadcasts would owe their appearance in it to the mere accident of their placing. Viewers were notoriously disinclined to switch to another channel after seeing a show so that if, say, a news bulletin followed immediately after a programme which qualified for the Top Twenty it would stand a good chance of making the grade too. That this was in effect accidental would be demonstrated the next night when the News audience was much smaller simply because it had followed a programme with a limited appeal.

Then there was the fact that 'getting into the Top Twenty' – or scraping into one of the last few places in it – was to some extent a matter of pure luck. While there might be no doubt which were the top fifteen, there could well be a large number of programmes jostling for the last five of the coveted twenty places. There might be no statistically significant difference between the estimates of their audiences so that those which made the grade would do so by mere chance.

If the Top Twenty had been taken no more seriously than What The Stars Foretell, none of these objections would have been worth bothering about. But there was plenty of evidence that all too many in the broadcasting business – producers and, even more, artists – took them very seriously indeed, some no doubt because they were naive but others because they saw them heeded by people in a position to make vital decisions. I had myself seen in the U.S.A. the almost superstitious reverence with which the announcements of the Top Twenty were greeted. If you were 'In' you were euphoric; if you were 'Out' you were in despair. And if you never were 'In' – and should you be responsible for anything but a popular show you never could be 'In' – you were a second class citizen in the world of broadcasting. I like to think that the BBC's refusal to publish Top Twenties did something to prevent their worst effects here.

The Survey's findings about the outcome of competition up to the time when the BBC was allowed to open a second service (BBC-2) are set out in two tables below. The first relates to the growth in, and change in the character of, the Television Public. It will be recalled that in order to receive ITV the viewer had either to have his receiver adapted so that he could tune in to Band III on which it was broadcast or else buy a two-channel receiver. It was inevitably some time before the Independent Television Authority completed its network of transmitters so that its service could be seen by all viewers everywhere hence, as the first table shows, it was about nine years before all television sets could receive both BBC and ITV programmes. In the meantime, the normal growth of the Television Public was continuing: from being 40 per cent of the population in 1955 it rose to 89 per cent by the end of 1963. (It was sometimes said that the coming of ITV accelerated this expansion. In fact, the curve of growth proceeded at the same rate as it had done during the monopoly era and there is no reason to suppose that it would not have done so even if the BBC's had continued to be the only television service.)

SIZE OF THE TELEVISION PUBLIC, OCT.-DEC. 1955–63

Proportion of the population* having:

	single channel receivers (a)	two channel receivers (b)	Total with TV (c)	no TV receivers (d)	Grand Total (e)	(b) as % of (c)
	%	%	%	%	%	%
1955	35	5	40	60	100	12
1956	30	18	48	52	100	38
1957	31	25	56	44	100	45
1958	20	45	65	35	100	69
1959	14	61	75	25	100	81
1960	10	72	82	18	100	88
1961	5	80	85	15	100	94
1962	4	84	88	12	100	95
1963	2	87	89	11	100	98

* 1955–56 excluding children under 16; 1956 *et seq.* excluding children under 5.

The second table shows the quantity of viewing year by year and the way in which two-channel viewing was shared between BBC and ITV. The length of time which was spent in viewing amounted to between one and a half and nearly two hours an evening, increasing as transmission times were extended. It is significant that people who could view either BBC or ITV spent little, if any, more time in viewing than did those who could only watch BBC. In the first quarter shown, October–December 1955, which was also the first quarter of ITV broadcasting, BBC-TV had the lion's share, the ratio being 54 : 46. But this was not maintained. A year later the balance had swung to BBC 38 : ITV 62 and in 1957 and 1958 the BBC's share was only one third. The pendulum swung again in 1961, coinciding with a new look in BBC-TV (*Steptoe, Z-cars, Maigret, That Was The Week That Was*, etc.) introduced under the new BBC-TV management of Stuart Hood and the dynamic, if abrasive, young Donald Baverstock. The following year what had generally come to be considered impossible happened: there was a ratio of 50:50.

QUANTITY OF VIEWING, OCT.-DEC. 1955–63

Daily average in the evening* per head of population with TV†

	Of BBC by single-channel public	By the two-channel public			Two-channel ratio
		BBC	ITV	Total	
	hrs mins	h: m	h: m	h: m	BBC: ITV
1955	1: 34	0: 50	0: 43	1: 33	54: 46
1956	1: 37	0: 35	1: 06	1: 41	38: 62
1957	1: 41	0: 34	1: 07	1: 41	34: 66
1958	1: 41	0: 36	1: 11	1: 47	34: 66
1959	1: 41	0: 40	1: 03	1: 43	39: 61
1960	1: 54	0: 43	1: 13	1: 45	37: 63
1961	1: 56	0: 51	1: 04	1: 55	44: 56
1962	1: 53	0: 57	0: 57	1: 54	50: 50
1963	1: 50	0: 51	1: 01	1: 52	45: 55

* 1955–6, 7.00–11.00 p.m.; 1957 *et seq.* 6.00–11.00 p.m.

† 1955–59, excluding children under 16; 1960 *et seq.* excluding children under 5

It should, of course, be borne in mind that while the two-channel public remained small and, as a consequence, the overwhelming majority of the Television Public had no choice but to view BBC programmes, the BBC's *total* audiences were only marginally reduced by defections to ITV. Thus even in October-December 1957, when the two-channel public had risen to 45 per cent of the Television Public and the ratio stood at 34:66, the BBC's *total* audiences were still, on the average, more than twice as big as those of ITV. The passing of the years eliminated this handicap so that by 1963 the two-channel ratio virtually represented the distribution of *all* viewing.

We learned more about the Television Public from a special 'bench-mark' inquiry (subsequently published by the BBC as *The Public and the Programmes*). It was conducted in 1958 when about two-thirds of the population had TV-sets, 20 per cent single-channel and 45 per cent two-channel, and the BBC:ITV ratio stood at 34:66. Two-channel families, we found, tended to include more children and fewer over 60s and also a smaller proportion of people with higher education than their numbers warranted.

As to their viewing, the inquiry showed there to be a considerable dispersion around the mean of about one and three-quarter hours per head each evening. One in six viewed, on the average, for less than an hour a night while at the other extreme another sixth viewed for three or more hours. Nearly 40 per cent of the two-channel public admitted that they were 'not very choosey' about what they watched. About one-third virtually confined their viewing to one service and this was far more often ITV than BBC. Among the rest, who divided their custom, the more an individual viewed and the less choosey he admitted himself to be, the more likely was he to prefer ITV to BBC programmes. In particular, the young and those in semi- or unskilled occupations preferred ITV whereas the preference for BBC-TV was most marked among older people and among the professional and highly skilled.

The tastes of the ITV addicts, if that is the right way to describe them, were found to differ sharply from those of the addicts of BBC-TV. In particular the ITV addicts rated the following four types of programmes far more highly than did the BBC addicts: Westerns, Crime series, Comedy film series and Quizzes. The BBC addicts, on the other hand, rated these four types far more favourably than did the addicts of ITV: Documentaries, Science, Serious Music and Light Music programmes.

As soon as the BBC:ITV ratio seemed to have reached an equilibrium we started asking ourselves why it should have stabilised at this particular point. It would have been reasonable to expect the two-channel public to have divided their custom fairly equally had the introduction of competitive television appeared to them to be analogous to the opening of a rival multiple store selling much the same goods at much the same prices as the one which was there already. But the fact that far more chose to view ITV than chose to view BBC called for an explanation. Why did they show this preference? There were plenty of guesses, but few facts in the early days.

Gradually the picture came into focus. Within a few months of ITV's inauguration we were reporting, on the basis of a comparative study of what viewers thought of particular BBC and ITV programmes they had watched, that there was no evidence that viewers considered individual ITV programmes any 'better', each for each, than the BBC's. A few months later the *News-Chronicle* published a Gallup Poll which on superficial reading, seemed to contradict this. It showed that, of six types of programme, there was only one, Variety, which the public thought that ITV 'did better' than BBC-TV. They thought that BBC-TV 'did better than ITV' with Plays, Sporting events, News, Documentaries and Children's programmes. But these findings were susceptible of another explanation: that ITV's service was preferred because it devoted more of its time to Variety which was what a majority of the public most wanted from television.

In 1959 we tried the experiment of confronting a sample of two-channel viewers with a hundred adjectives, asking them to say which they thought applied to BBC-TV and which to ITV. But there was an ambiguity in the method. It made no provision for the viewer to say whether, in applying an adjective, he was intending it in praise or disparagement. Often the intention was obvious, but it was not always so. For example, which was meant when a viewer said a service was 'American', as many did say of ITV?

Two years later we made a more thorough attempt to delineate the current 'images' of BBC-TV and ITV. Between two and three thousand two-channel viewers took part. They were shown forty adjectives and had to say which ones described what they liked about BBC-TV (and later ITV) and which described what they disliked about them. At the same time we collected information about the viewers' actual behaviour so that the images they held could be related to whether they predominantly viewed BBC or ITV.

One of the adjectives which was generally agreed to describe a desirable attribute of a television service, 'entertaining', was applied just about as often to BBC-TV as to ITV. Others of them, such as 'educational', 'adult', 'responsible' and 'dignified', were applied more often to BBC-TV and some, such as 'free-and-easy', 'informal', 'matey' and 'modern', more often to ITV.

On the other hand adjectives which were generally thought to denote undesirable attributes included, as well as the obvious ones like 'dull', 'heavy' and 'boring' (which were applied more often to BBC-TV), 'money-making', 'childish', 'bitty' and 'American' (which were applied more often to ITV).

But in the main the images of both BBC-TV and ITV, though different, were favourable and significantly the BBC-inclined and the ITV-inclined viewers were largely in agreement in the way they conceived the two services. Where they differed seemed to be more in the importance they attached to the qualities they agreed as being either attractive or repellent.

Later, though before the 1961–2 swing to BBC-TV, these results were incorporated with others in a systematic examination of the dynamics of 'channel choice' (subsequently written up in *New Society* as *What Makes Viewers Choose*, Silvey and Emmett, 14th March, 1963). This led to the conclusion that while a preference for the output of a service is *one* of the reasons why people view it more

'. . . it is rarely the *only* reason and in many cases it does not apply at all. There was little evidence to suggest that people were deterred from viewing BBC-TV because they had an unfavourable image of it (alongside a favourable image of ITV). Some BBC-inclined viewers, but not many, were put off by an unfavourable image of ITV. Most people seemed to have predominantly favourable, or indifferent, images of both services. The quality of reception seemed seldom to determine viewing behaviour nor did the need to adjust the controls on the set seem to deter many viewers from switching from one service to another.

'But a desire for undemanding entertainment, coupled with feeling that that was what ITV could be relied upon to supply, did appear to activate an appreciable number of ITV-inclined viewers. And one motive which did appear to activate some BBC-inclined viewers was a cordial dislike of TV commercials. However there did not seem to be many – except among the most avid viewers of BBC – who were so satisfied with the comprehensiveness of the service of their choice that they saw no need to try viewing the other.

'Sheer ignorance of what the "other channel" had to offer, which could be a reason for not viewing it, was uncommon. It was found that a very high proportion of viewers were not always their own masters in the matter of programme choice, for there were the wishes of others in the family to be considered. Clearly, this could distort the "free play of the market". Finally, the tendency for the viewer to conform, in the business of channel-choice, to the mores of his group emerged as one of the motives activating a minority of viewers and this applied far more often to the ITV-inclined than to the BBC-inclined.'

With this analysis as a tool, even if not a perfect one, for understanding the factors which determined channel choice, and with accumulating evidence that when BBC programmes and ITV programmes catered for the same needs viewers were as happy with one as with the other, the outlines of an explanation of the BBC one-third:ITV two-thirds distribution of the public's custom, which seemed so immutable in the first few years of competition, became clearer. Viewers had learned that the kind of undemanding entertainment, which for most of them was their primary requirement of television, was to be found in greater abundance on ITV than on BBC-TV. In a word, it was the character of ITV's *programme mix* which tilted the scales.

But if that were so, what accounted for the swing to BBC-TV in 1961–2? It would be difficult to demonstrate that the BBC had revised its own mix, making it more like that of ITV. In my view, BBC-TV's new management achieved the same end by the more subtle means of infusing new life into its output so that, though still clearly distinguishable from the output of ITV, it was in its own distinct way just as entertaining. A new situation was created when permission to open a second channel was granted to the BBC but withheld from ITV. This will be discussed in the next chapter.

Meantime the increased complexity of our daily Survey lead us with inexorable logic to data processing by computer. In this we were pioneers within the Corporation – and paid the inevitable price of having to endure the teething troubles. I thankfully left the transitional arrangements to Emmett who had been tireless in his advocacy of, pace the word, computerisation and maintained his faith even when the service bureau on which at first we relied nearly drove us demented by falling disastrously behind its time-schedule. Eventually the BBC acquired its own computer, first for its salary computations and later for a multitude of other purposes, so we had to take on our own departmental systems analysts and programmers. By this time I was beginning to feel I was too old to learn new tricks and was content to abide by the advice of the experts on what could, and could not, be done. But I did learn by bitter experience that a computer is no more than a high-speed moron and that as a moron can't be expected to assume anything it must be given meticulous instructions (programmes) which can take a very, very long time to write.

The Audience Research Department had by then a new home: The Langham, an immense Victorian pile commanding from its face a magnificent view up one of London's noblest streets, Portland Place. Its inside-walls were at least two and a half feet thick which made a built-in cupboard in my room so capacious that my daughter pointed out that I could comfortably conceal within it anyone with whom I did not wish an unexpected caller to discover me. But I told her that that would have been inconsistent with the unassailable respectability of its history. It had previously been London's first luxury hotel, a safe haven for the wives and daughters of visiting provincial bishops. It had many distinctions: when it opened it took pride in its new 'vertical railways'; it soon housed H. M. Stanley while he recruited companions for another expedition to Darkest Africa; it was the birthplace of the father of my colleague Michael Standing and it was long the home of the novelist Ouida whose sole claim to immortality seems to rest upon her famous line: 'All rowed fast but none rowed faster than stroke.'

In the last days of the fifties I received a communication from 10 Downing St telling me of the Prime Minister's intention to submit my name to the Palace for an award of O.B.E.

This was a complete surprise. I knew, of course, that this suggestion could only have emanated from the BBC itself and that as the quota for such awards for Corporation staff inevitably fell far short of the number of deserving cases, my selection was to that extent a matter of chance. Nevertheless I was genuinely gratified, feeling it to be as much a recognition of my department's contribution to broadcasting as a personal award. And I was touched by the tone of the letters of congratulation which reached me when the 1960 New Year's Honours List was published. One man, whom I had always known as a sceptic of audience research, wrote '. . . if the point of such things is the recognition of long and devoted service, then for once its good to see they've picked the right person'.

Like everyone else who has had to attend an investiture, I was enormously impressed by the unobtrusive efficiency with which the operation was carried out. My family, ensconsed with all the other admiring relations in the Buckingham Palace ballroom, watched with fascination the venerable Gentlemen-At-Arms marching slowly down the aisles, with relief when they finally took up their positions on the dais and with delight when the Band of the Brigade of Guards, which had been playing selections from 'My Fair Lady' in the gallery, then broke into 'We never thought you'd do it, you'd do it, you'd do it'.

Thinking it possible that the monarch might ask me what I 'did', I had prepared myself with an answer; I would reply 'I am in the BBC, Ma'am.' In the event the question came and I gave my carefully rehearsed reply, but then came an unexpected supplementary: 'Yes, but what do you do there?' This called for quick thinking for an adequate answer, I had long found, took forty minutes. So I said 'Well among other things I find out how many people listen to you, Ma'am'. To which to my surprise the monarch replied with a smile: 'Oh, Audience Research, eh?' thus showing herself either to be very well briefed or better informed than 99.9 per cent of her subjects, or both.

A few years later another award, the M.B.E., was bestowed on a member of Audience Research's staff, Mrs Norah Gaetjens, who had joined us after her husband was killed by a bomb which fell on Broadcasting House in 1940 and who had ever since carried out with efficiency and devotion important, but not very exciting, duties. Once again the general feeling was that They 'had picked the right person'. But I think she derived almost as much pleasure from the fact that among those attending the same investiture were The Beatles.

12 Post-Pilkington

This final chapter deals with the 1960s, the years which were, for me, the last lap of my service as H.A.R. By the time the decade opened the established staff of the Audience Research Department was about one hundred – a far cry from the one-man-and-a-girl of 1936. But I never felt that the mere fact of having a fairly big staff was anything to get puffed-up about; indeed, there were times when I found myself envying the departments that needed no more than a cosy dozen or so to do all that had to be done.

My department was organised in six sections. Two of them were concerned with the continuous Survey of Listening and Viewing: the *Fieldwork Section* recruited and trained interviewers, set them to work, audited their performance and in due course paid them off; the *Statistics Section* prepared the daily log-sheets which the interviewers used in the field, processed the data collected, punching the cards (and later the computer tapes) and preparing the daily Barometers, daily audience charts and other tabulations. Two more sections were concerned with the panels which provided information about audiences' reactions to programmes: *Registry and Records* looked after their recruitment and staffing, kept their files and sorted the weekly inflow of completed questionnaires; the *Analysis Section* drafted the questionnaires and coped with them when they were completed, tabulating the answers, assessing written comment and preparing the final reports. *Projects and Developments* – essentially a 'jobbing' activity – was the fifth section while the sixth was the *Information Desk* which was responsible for the dessemination of reports, keeping the departmental archives and dealing with the constant inflow of telephone and written inquiries.

There was a lot to do. The *Fieldwork Section* had to nourish a pool of interviewers which had to be kept up to a strength of some 1,300. The *Statistics Section* had to punch about one and a half million cards a year and produce the daily Barometers within a week or so of the days to which they related. *Registry and Records*, besides ensuring that the panels were kept up to their established strengths, had to handle an influx of something like three-quarters of a million documents a year while the *Anlysis Section* had to draft questionnaires and prepare reports on an annual total of about 3,000 different broadcasts.

Every Tuesday morning my deputy and I met to review progress. Section Heads would join us as appropriate (they were free to sit-in for the whole meeting, but usually preferred to get back to their desks when their own business had been disposed of). Progress on current projects usually took up much of the morning since the Survey and the Panels, being routine, largely looked after themselves. At noon the Administrative Officer of the Division of which Audience Research was part would join us to discuss matters like recruitment, grading, and promotion of staff.

Recruitment was a perpetual headache. Departments had no power to negotiate about salaries; these were determined by the grades of the posts. These grades had been previously approved by Organisation and Management, a central department, and many were the battles which grading caused. Since departments felt sure that they, and only they, knew what a job involved while O. & M. had to ensure that all BBC jobs of equal responsibility were graded equally, the opportunities for disagreement were endless.

As one of the less glamourous departments, we were handicapped in our recruitment of secretaries. Bright young women thought secretarial work in the BBC as an affair of studios, contact with artists and vicarious participation in expense account jaunts, rather than in the meticulous typing of statistical tables. In recruiting – and retaining – senior research staff we were up against the competition of market researchers, often the adjuncts of wealthy advertising agencies, who could afford to pay salaries far above those which a public corporation could offer.

Our Tuesday morning meetings were quite informal. We

met in my office, I at my desk with my secretary minuting decisions at my side and everyone else in easy chairs. We never took a vote. The final responsibility was mine but I rarely had to say we would follow a course of action with ran counter to the advice of a sectional head immediately concerned.

Wednesday was the day for regular contact with the various planners. Between us my deputy and I would see or 'phone each of them to take up any point about current findings, to hear of the plans they had in mind and to agree upon which future programmes should be the subject of reaction reports. Programme Planners came and went fairly frequently – planning was a step towards Higher Things – so during my time these meetings brought me into fairly intimate contact with many, some of whom later became highly influential within the BBC though they were rarely familiar figures to the public.

Among those whom I particularly recall was Godfrey Adams who succeeded Charles Siepmann as planner of the war-time Home Service and Forces Programme. It was during one of our weekly meetings, in June 1940, that the news of the French capitulation came through. Godfrey's laconic comment was characteristic: 'Now perhaps we can get on with the war unhampered by our Allies.' There was Harman Grisewood, who looked what he was, a Catholic intellectual. On first acquaintance one could be forgiven for thinking that this gentle, scholarly man might have little knowledge of, or skill in, practical affairs; in fact when later he became *eminence grise* to Hugh Greene as Director-General he was to prove one of the shrewdest of advisers. There was the inexhaustible Norman Collins, who worked all day as hard as any man and retired at night to turn out best-selling novels and who later left the BBC to campaign with equal energy for commercial television. At Alexandra Palace in the first days of post-war television there was Maurice Gorham and later, at the new Television Centre, Stuart Hood, lovable but enigmatic who revealed some of his complex nature in an account of his war, *Pebbles in My Skull*. Another who combined planning with authorship was Howard Newby, then responsible for the Third Programme and now for all radio programmes.

Post-Pilkington 199

These weekly meetings were immensely helpful to us and, I hope, to the planners too. They seemed to enjoy testing out their ideas. If they sought advice it was given – though not necessarily followed, as was their right. In my considered view it was probably at these weekly meetings over the years that audience research had its greatest influence on BBC policy even though by far the greater part our findings had, of necessity, to be communicated in writing.

The quiverful of requests for audience reaction reports which we brought back from the planners were not the only ones we had to try to meet. The regional planners, in Bristol, Birmingham, Cardiff, Manchester, Glasgow and Belfast, each sent their demands in writing and output departments were entitled to indent too. No time could be lost for the questionnaires had to be dispatched to panel members within a few days. The first step, which was usually executed by my deputy, was to decide which requests it would be possible to meet, bearing in mind the limits of the panels' capacity. Compiling the weekly schedule of programmes to be the subject of individual inquiry was rather like designing a jig-saw puzzle under pressure. Once it was done it was discussed with the Head of the Analysis Section who was responsible for drafting the necessary questionnaires and getting them to our long-suffering printers. Mercifully over the years she had built up a bank of questions which between them met most needs but there was seldom a week in which new questions did not have to be designed and this called for very careful drafting.

Thursday was 'Bulletin day' – the day on which I drafted the weekly *Audience Research Bulletin* which was the pivotal vehicle for the internal dissemination of the department's work. Its standard contents consisted of a series of tables, updated each week, showing the trends in viewing and listening to each service at different times of day and in the various regions together with a brief commentary calling attention to significant changes. This was followed by Programme Notes in which a selection of broadcasts would be dealt with; each would show the broadcast's estimated audience, Reaction Index and give a verbal description of the reasons for the reception it had enjoyed. But these standard contents would be preceeded by varying 'opening paragraphs'. If we had issued any special report during the preceeding week we would advertise it here so as to make its existence known as widely as possible and also whet the appetite of those who had received it but wearily put it in their Pending Tray to be read, hopefully, *sometime*. Opening paragraphs might also deal with other organisations' researches, such as polls published by newspapers, journal articles and books relevant to audience research, or it might trail our own plans. Our aim was to make the *Bulletin* interesting and indispensible reading. To judge by the promptitude with which any misprint was called to our attention, some people did read it.

Special Numbers of the *Bulletin* were prepared at quarterly intervals. This gave us an opportunity to review trends and developments in a wider perspective and to deal at greater length with problems that were chronic rather than acute. The *Bulletin* had a wide circulation round the BBC – about 150 copies were distributed – but, as with all Audience Research documents, it could be shown or passed on to any member of staff.

Another regular chore for the departmental management, which came round once a month, was drafting the *Audience Research Newsletter*. The *Newsletter* had a circulation of several thousands; it went to all the Audience Research workers – Survey interviewers, panel members both active and standing by waiting to be called on for active service and to all members of our own headquarters staff. Its intention was to keep them in the picture by telling them of the findings of audience research to which they had in their various ways contributed and, indeed, of other research matter which we thought might interest them. It was necessarily written in an informal style, avoiding technicalities and, since it was a letter, was personally signed. It was labelled 'Confidential' mainly, I must confess, in order to make the recipients feel they were getting something that other people weren't, for we avoided including anything which would have been embarrassing had it 'leaked' which, surprisingly, it seldom did.

Besides correspondence – mostly internal – *ad hoc* meetings, staff training lectures, attending appointments boards and getting to know new staff, much of the rest of my time was spent in drafting reports or in editing the drafts of others. I attached great importance to the style – and to the appearance – of audience research reports for it was by them that in large measure our activities were judged. Inevitably much of our work was quantitative, but we had to accept the fact that numeracy was less common than literacy. Our reports had to be lucid, but they also had to be readable. Precision was essential, so sometimes terms had to be exactly defined, but jargon was anathema. (The famous example from the American Census, the table headed 'U.S. Population Broken Down by Age and Sex', stood as an awful warning.)

Although it could never be right for us to show as a finding of our researches anything that we had not in fact found, I felt we need not be inhibited from speculating, indeed it could be a duty to speculate, about what we had discovered and to suggest the conclusions to which by induction they pointed; always provided it was made perfectly clear where fact ended and speculation began. And as we had always to remember that our recipients all had much else to read, prolixity was a deadly sin.

All this meant that it sometimes took an inordinate time to draft a single paragraph to one's satisfaction. But I must confess that if I did finally succeed in expressing a difficult thought with what seemed to me to be clarity I found the experience to be as profoundly satisfying as it was mortifying to discover subsequently that some reader didn't understand what I was getting at.

The Beveridge Committee, sitting shortly after the war, reviewed a monopoly BBC; a monopoly which, almost despite themselves, they had recommended should be continued in the public interest. But before the Labour government could put this recommendation into effect it had been replaced by a Conservative government and by 1955 Independent Television was an accomplished fact. The next decennial review, by the Pilkington Committee, had therefore to scrutinise the performance of ITV as well as the BBC and its report was eagerly awaited.

I appeared before Pilkington as a witness, as I had before

Beveridge, and while others of my colleagues were being cross-examined I noticed that one of the Committee's members, Miss Joyce Grenfell, seemed to be making particularly copious notes. It was only afterwards that another member, Richard Hoggart, told me that she was busy on her regular task of providing the rest of the Committee with a lightning sketch of each witness. (I subsequently taxed Miss Grenfell with this saying that I was sure I had escaped because she had never looked my way. Her reply was an enigmatic but emphatic 'Oh yes I did').

The Pilkington report was gratifying in its reference to Audience Research. It said: 'The BBC should continue to engage in continuous and perceptive audience research, which should continue to command the resources reasonably needed.' The recommendation which interested the public most concerned the allocation of further television channels. Both sides wanted one. The BBC had argued that with only one channel it was impossible to provide the quality of television service which viewers were entitled to expect from a national broadcasting authority; if they had a second they would use it to extend the range of their output and in particular to broadcast types of programme for which previously there had been no space. Pilkington accepted these arguments and recommended that the BBC should be empowered to provide a second service but that, at any rate for the time being, the ITA should not.

Shortly afterwards a Gallup Poll was published which showed that nearly three-quarters of the population said that they had 'read or heard about' the Pilkington report (a high proportion) and that half the population were prepared to express an opinion on the work the Committee had done. Thirty per cent thought it had done 'a good job' and less than 20 per cent took the opposite view. As to the recommendation that the BBC should have a second channel, nearly two-thirds approved and only 19 per cent disapproved. After the announcement of the Government's decisions – which followed the Pilkington recommendations about further channels – another Gallup Poll showed 63 per cent in favour of a second channel for BBC-TV but 45 per cent *against* the decision to withhold a second channel from the ITA.

Existing television sets would not, however, be able to receive the new service for it was to be broadcast on Ultra High Frequency wavelengths (UHF). There was no question, as there was when ITV began, of existing sets being adaptable; new sets would have to be acquired (either by purchase or, more likely, by hire).

The new service, BBC-2, went on the air in the Autumn of 1964 and it was not long before it was clear that the public was in no great hurry to re-equip themselves to receive it. As the table below shows, at the beginning of its third year only 13 per cent of the television public could receive BBC-2 and at the beginning of its sixth year this proportion had still not reached 50 per cent. This was in striking contrast to the rate at which viewers had equipped themselves to receive ITV programmes. At the beginning of ITV's third year the 'two-channel public' had amounted to 45 per cent and at the beginning of its sixth, nearly 90 per cent.

SIZE OF THE TELEVISION PUBLIC, OCT.-DEC. 1964–69

Proportion of the population (excluding children under 5) able to receive:

	BBC-1 and ITV only (a)	BBC-1, BBC-2 and ITV (b)	Total with TV (c)	No TV receiver (d)	Grand Total (e)	(b) as % of (c)
	%	%	%	%	%	
1964	88	3	91	9	100	3
1965	84	8	92	8	100	9
1966	81	12	93	7	100	13
1967	70	23	93	7	100	25
1968	61	32	93	7	100	34
1969	51	42	93	7	100	45

The next table shows how those who *had* acquired UHF receivers divided their time between the three services, BBC-1, BBC-2 and ITV, which were thus available to them. From the start they devoted only about one-tenth of their viewing to BBC-2. To be sure there were occasions when large numbers of them viewed BBC-2, but these were noticeably confined to the times when it transmitted such predictable audience-pullers as

The High Chapparal and even these audiences were less than such shows would have drawn had they been transmitted on BBC-1 or ITV.

QUANTITY OF VIEWING, OCT.-DEC. 1964–72

Daily average during BBC-2 transmission hours per head of population with UHF-TV sets (excluding children under 5)

	BBC-1	BBC-2	ITV	Total	Ratio
	hrs mins	hrs mins	hrs mins	hrs mins	BBC-1:BBC-2:ITV
1964	0 : 42	0 : 10	0 : 48	1 : 40	42 : 10 : 48
1965	0 : 44	0 : 10	0 : 48	1 : 40	44 : 8 : 48
1966	0 : 44	0 : 10	0 : 48	1 : 40	44 : 8 : 48
1967	0 : 42	0 : 10	0 : 47	1 : 39	42 : 10 : 48
1968	0 : 48	0 : 12	0 : 39	1 : 39	48 : 12 : 39
1969	0 : 38	0 : 12	0 : 46	1 : 36	40 : 12 : 48
1970	0 : 43	0 : 10	0 : 43	1 : 36	45 : 10 : 45
1971	0 : 40	0 : 12	0 : 45	1 : 37	41 : 13 : 46
1972	0 : 43	0 : 11	0 : 31	1 : 35	47 : 11 : 42

There can be little doubt that to some extent viewers' tardiness in acquiring UHF sets and the modest extent to which those who had done so actually used them to view BBC-2 owes something to the fact that BBC-2 acquired for many a somewhat 'highbrow' image, if only because it included programmes not previously shown on BBC-1 for lack of sufficient general appeal. All the same it was difficult to resist the impression that for many viewers two alternatives were as much as they wanted – or perhaps as much as they could cope with – and that, faced with a choice of three, they were almost bewildered.

There is little evidence to suggest that, once people could get three services instead of two, they spent more time in viewing. (There was similarly little evidence that the availability of two services instead of one caused people to view more.) But if viewing per head does not increase as services multiply, some service must suffer. When ITV first appeared on the scene, the bulk of its audiences were people who would otherwise have been viewing BBC-TV (the rest were new viewers). The source from which BBC-2's audiences were drawn is harder to identify with certainty because other variables were present, but it seems likely that more were diverted from BBC-1 than from ITV. Be that as it may, the table below shows how the quantity of evening viewing, and its distribution between BBC-TV (1 and 2) and ITV, up to the time when colour became a factor to be reckoned with.

QUANTITY OF VIEWING, OCT.-DEC. 1964–68

Daily average between 6.00 and 11.00 p.m. per head of population with TV (excluding children under 5)

	BBC-TV (-1 and -2)	ITV	Total	Ratio
	hrs mins	hrs mins	hrs mins	BBC : ITV
1964	0 : 51	1 : 00	1 : 51	46 : 54
1965	0 : 49	0 : 57	1 : 46	46 : 54
1966	0 : 55	0 : 57	1 : 52	49 : 51
1967	0 : 55	0 : 58	1 : 53	49 : 51
1968	0 : 64	0 : 49	1 : 53	57 : 43

Another 'bench-mark' inquiry, carried out in 1967, threw light on the changes of which had taken place in the distribution of viewing during the previous decade, as these figures show:

	Proportions of those who could view both BBC-TV and ITV		
	1967	1961	1958
Viewed:	%	%	%
BBC exclusively	2	9	9
BBC more than ITV	33	25	17
The 'BBC-inclined'	35	34	26
BBC and ITV about equally	19	8	8
ITV more than BBC	35	40	32
ITV exclusively	5	16	24
The 'ITV-inclined'	40	56	56
No information	6	2	10
	100	100	100

People who viewed one service to the exclusion of the other were a diminishing band. The BBC-inclined had grown, the

ITV-inclined had shrunk and those who divided their time evenly had more than doubled.

The age-distribution of the BBC-inclined had changed: by 1967 it was no longer heavily over-weighted with the elderly but had drawn close to that of the population. The age-composition of the ITV-inclined, too, now resembled that of the population as a whole, being no longer disproportionately young (though ITV still kept its strong hold on the teenagers). But the social differences between the BBC- and the ITV-inclined still remained. The majority of those with most education or higher occupational status were BBC-inclined, but not so those with low occupational status or minimal education. Sixty-one per cent of the readers of *The Times* and of *The Guardian* and 51 per cent of the readers of the *Daily Telegraph* were BBC-inclined as compared with only 27 per cent of the readers of the *Daily Mirror*. Compared with the ITV-inclined, the BBC-inclined tended to be more choosey about the programmes they viewed, to spend less time in viewing and to be prepared to face a break-down in their TV-sets with greater equanimity. (While we were writing up these findings the seven-year-old son of one of our panel members came home from school singing:

> 'While shepherds watched their flocks by night
> They had on ITV
> An angel of the Lord came down
> And switched to BBC')

The table showing the quantity of viewing in 1969–72 relates to the period from 7.30 to 11.00 p.m. It shows that the amount of viewing per head was substantially constant over these four years though its distribution between BBC and ITV gave the BBC a clear lead in the last three.

The prospect of being able to receive colour television was a shot in the arm for the sale of UHF sets. As the next table shows, by the autumn of 1970 a majority of viewers could receive BBC-2 as well as BBC-1 and ITV and that two years later three out of four could see all three services. At the time of writing the rate at which viewers are acquiring colour television sets appears to be faster than that at which they

QUANTITY OF VIEWING, OCT.-DEC. 1969–72

*Daily average between 7.30 and 11.00 p.m.
per head of population with TV (excluding children under 5)*

	BBC-TV (-1 and -2)	ITV	Total	Ratio
	hrs mins	hrs mins	hrs mins	BBC:ITV
1969	0 : 46	0 : 48	1 : 34	49 : 51
1970	0 : 51	0 : 44	1 : 35	53 : 47
1971	0 : 49	0 : 47	1 : 36	52 : 48
1972	0 : 53	0 : 41	1 : 34	57 : 43

acquired UHF. The table also shows that by the end of 1972 17 per cent of the television public could receive their programmes in colour.

SIZE OF THE TELEVISION PUBLIC, OCT.-DEC. 1970–2

Proportion of the population (excluding children under 5) able to receive:

	BBC-1 & ITV only	BBC-1, BBC-2 & ITV	in mono-chrome	in colour	Total with TV	no TV receiver	Grand Total
	%	%	%	%	%	%	%
1970	43	51	91	3	94	6	100
1971	31	64	87	8	95	5	100
1972	18	77	78	17	95	5	100

Finally, do viewers who can see their television in colour view more than those who can only see them in monochrome? It is too early to be certain for only figures for October–December 1972 are available at the time of writing. They are set out below.

COMPARISON OF THE QUANTITY OF VIEWING OF THOSE WITH/WITHOUT COLOUR RECEIVERS

Daily average per head, out of a possible 8 hours, 20 minutes

Viewers able to receive all three services:	BBC-1	BBC-2	ITV	Total	Ratio
	hrs mins	hrs mins	hrs mins	hrs mins	BBC-1:BBC-2:ITV
in Colour	1 : 18	0 : 13	1 : 02	2 : 31	51 : 9 : 40
in Monochrome	1 : 11	0 : 11	1 : 04	2 : 26	47 : 8 : 45

At any rate in these three months BBC-TV, but not ITV, was viewed more by those with colour receivers than by those with monochrome only, hence the distribution of the viewing of the colour-owners was more favourable to BBC-TV than was that of the owners of other UHF sets.

Turning from television to radio, it will be seen from the table below that the quantity of listening to BBC Radio between 9.00 a.m. and 11.00 p.m. diminished year by year from 1948 to 1960. In 1948 it was two hours forty minutes per day per head (out of a possible sixteen hours). In 1957 it was only half as much and by 1960 it had fallen to one hour six minutes. Thereafter it fluctuated between one hour five minutes and one hour sixteen minutes a day. But the trend in the daytime (9.00 a.m. – 6.00 p.m.) was very different from that in the evening (6.00 – 11.00 p.m.). Daytime listening, which was one hour nineteen minutes (out of a possible nine hours) in 1948, reached its nadir in 1958 and then revived, to reach one hour two minutes in 1970. Evening listening, on the other hand, dropped steadily from one hour twenty-one minutes (out of a possible five hours) in 1948 to a mere ten minutes or less after 1963. The explanation lies, of course, in the spread of television. As soon as a family acquired a television set it reduced its listening, that in the evening drastically, but that in the daytime much less so partly because daytime television programmes were limited but more because the day's work had to be done and, though it may be possible to listen while you work, viewing and working are for most people incompatible.

Although the quantity of evening listening *per head of population* had become derisory by the sixties, this did not mean that evening radio audiences were negligible. Ten minutes of listening per head of population was equivalent to a constant audience of one and a half million people. These evening radio audiences consisted of two groups: those still without television sets and those who, for one reason or another, listened to radio in preference to viewing television. Of course as the years passed the former, who listened much more than the latter, dwindled in number.

QUANTITY OF LISTENING TO BBC RADIO, OCT.-DEC. 1948–70
Daily average per head of population*

	Between 7 a.m. & 6 p.m.	Between 6 & 11 p.m.	Total
	hrs mins	hrs mins	hrs mins
1948	1 : 19	1 : 21	2 : 40
1949	1 : 10	1 : 14	2 : 24
1950	1 : 09	1 : 09	2 : 18
1951	1 : 08	1 : 04	2 : 12
1952	1 : 07	1 : 01	2 : 08
1953	0 : 55	0 : 50	1 : 45
1954	0 : 55	0 : 45	1 : 40
1955	0 : 53	0 : 39	1 : 32
1956	0 : 52	0 : 38	1 : 30
1957	0 : 51	0 : 29	1 : 20
1958	0 : 49	0 : 26	1 : 15
1959	0 : 50	0 : 21	1 : 11
1960	0 : 52	0 : 14	1 : 06
1961	0 : 55	0 : 12	1 : 07
1962	1 : 03	0 : 11	1 : 14
1963	1 : 04	0 : 10	1 : 14
1964	1 : 01	0 : 08	1 : 09
1965	0 : 58	0 : 07	1 : 05
1966	0 : 58	0 : 07	1 : 05
1967	1 : 08	0 : 08	1 : 16
1968	1 : 04	0 : 08	1 : 12
1969	1 : 04	0 : 08	1 : 12
1970	1 : 02	0 : 10	1 : 12

* 1948–59 excluding under 16
1960 *et seq.* excluding under 5

These trends demonstrated a reversal of radio's roles. Its predominant role – as a source of entertainment during hours of leisure – was increasingly assumed by television, but its subordinate role – as an accompaniment to other activities – remained and, indeed, increased in importance with the coming of the transistor set. Thus what had been radio's secondary, became its primary, role. That this meant that radio continued to serve a majority of the population could easily be demonstrated from the findings of the Survey. We made a practice of recording each day the proportion of the population that had made *any* use of the radio (regardless of how much). We called this radio's 'patronage'. The records showed that every day since the War BBC Radio's patronage had exceeded 50 per cent of the population and, of course, had we been able to record the proportion which made any use of radio over, say, a week, it would have been considerably higher.

Another by-product of the Survey gave a broad measure of the BBC's standing in the public's estimation. Every interview about 'yesterday's listening' was rounded off by the same question: 'On the whole are you satisfied or dissatisfied with current BBC programmes?' The informant could be put down as either 'Completely satisfied', 'Moderately satisfied' or 'Thoroughly dissatisfied'. We compiled an Index Number from the answers which we called the BBC Thermometer – because it measured 'temperature' rather than 'pressure'. Its maximum was $+100$ and its minimum -100.

The daily thermometer readings were astonishingly consistent, always falling within a narrow band from about $+65$ to about $+75$. Reassuringly, they showed no signs of falling off as listening declined, the 'thoroughly dissatisfied' never rising above 5 per cent. Two published Gallup Polls provided another piece of evidence which we learned of only when we read about them in the *News Chronicle*. Their question was 'Should the BBC continue its monopoly of radio in this country or should we also have commercial broadcasting paid for by advertisers?'. When they asked this question in 1946, and despite the tempting bait of 'paid for by advertisers', 44 per cent voted for a continuance of the monopoly, 43 per cent for commercial radio and 13 per cent expressed no opinion. But when three years later, in 1949, the same question was put again, the vote for the BBC's monopoly had risen to 51 per cent and the vote for commercial broadcasting had fallen to 33 per cent.

When the pattern of peace-time radio was first set up – in August 1945 – the Home Service, reconstituted on a regional basis, and the Light Programme were listened to about equally in the evening. But it was not long before Light Programme listening was considerably the greater. By the time the Third Programme came into being in 1946, an equilibrium had been established, the quantity of evening listening to the Light Programme being very nearly twice that of the Home Service. This remained substantially unchanged for the next twenty years. Because of its character, the Third Programme had a very restricted market hence listening to it *per head of population* was always marginal. It was however at much less of a disadvantage *vis à vis* the other services when the comparison was in terms of 'patronage', i.e. the numbers of people who *ever* listened to them.

The 'bench-mark' inquiry of 1958 (*The Public and the Programmes*) showed that among those who still lacked television about 40 per cent confined their BBC evening listening to the Light Programme (or the Light Programme and Radio Luxemburg, the commercial station whose programmes were beamed to Britain). This group were disproportionately young people of limited education and in semi- or unskilled occupations. Another, but much smaller minority, about 10 per cent, confined their evening listening to the Home Service; they tended to be past middle-age, to have had higher education and to be in professional or highly skilled occupations. The other half tended to roam the dial, seeking what they wanted wherever it might be. Sometimes, as on Saturday nights when the Home Service was host to *Music Hall* and *Saturday Night Theatre*, Light Programme listening was much less than that of the Home Service, but more often it was the Light Programme which claimed the lion's share. Another bench-mark inquiry, in 1961, showed the position to be substantially unchanged.

Early in the sixties a new phenomenon had to be reckoned with: the pirate radio stations. The British public had long been able to listen to commercial radio. Before the war Radios Luxemburg and Normandie, ignoring international agreements about the allocation of scarce wavelengths, had broadcast commercially financed programmes to Britain which, especially on Sundays, had brought them very large audiences indeed. After the war Luxemburg resumed operations but its transmissions in English were limited to the evening hours and, having now to compete with the new Light Programme, it never amounted to a serious threat to the dominant position of the BBC. The pirates were a different matter. Operated from ships moored around the coast, they broadcast all day an uninterrupted stream of records of 'pop' music – which was something that the BBC had never done and, because of the resistance of the Musicians' Union, could not have done. The pirate-king (or queen) was Radio Caroline.

Towards the end of 1964 we laid on a large-scale inquiry about what we called *The Caroline Phenomenon*. Questions were put to a one thousand sample of the population aged 11+ living in the areas where Caroline could be heard. As many as one in five of them were identified as Caroline 'addicts', addicts being defined as those who, on their own admission, 'often switched on to Radio Caroline without bothering to find out what was on the BBC'. Half the addicts were teenagers and 70 per cent were under the age of 30; they were drawn from all social and educational levels, though proportionately rather less from the 'top' third, than from the 'bottom' two-thirds, of the population. In their television tastes they tended to be more ITV-minded than the rest of the population and to be less interested in programmes that 'gave you something to think about'. They were also much more likely than other listeners to be aware of the programme preferences of their friends, hence they were more open to the influence of the mores of their peers.

We calculated that the quantity of Caroline listening was about one-third that of the Light Programme; nearly all of it was background listening and about a quarter of it occurred in places of work. Since our day-to-day survey had shown no significant decline in Light Programme listening coincident with the rise of the pirates, we were not surprised to find positive evidence that Caroline listening was largely 'new' listening, not displacing but supplementing listening to the BBC.

The prevailing image of Caroline was of a 'lively' and 'cheerful' service – but the same adjectives were frequently applied to the Light Programme. Friendly feelings towards Caroline did not necessarily imply unfriendly feelings towards the BBC. Its addicts made it clear that if Caroline were to cease broadcasting they would be very upset but most of the public would simply be indifferent whereas they would be sorry if ever the Light Programme were to disappear. In short

Caroline was meeting a need that the BBC had neglected – the need of the young for a continuous stream of pop.

Pressures from a number of quarters – from musicians who saw their livelihood threatened, composers whose copyrights were being infringed, foreign broadcasting authorities who objected to the interference with the reception of their programmes and lawyers who pointed to Caroline's illegality – lead to Government action to suppress Caroline. At the same time the way was made easier for the BBC to fill the breach which the success of the pirates had exposed.

In the re-organisation which followed the Light Programme bifurcated into Radio 1, the answer to Caroline, and Radio 2, fulfilling the role previously played by the Light Programme. What had been the Music Programme in the daytime and the Third Programme in the evening became Radio 3. The Home Service was re-christened Radio 4; later it was to lose its regional character and to become the primary vehicle for News and other 'spoken word' material.

A new pattern of listening soon established itself. About 40 per cent went to Radio 1, 35 per cent to Radio 2, 2 per cent to Radio 3, 20 per cent to Radio 4 and 3 per cent to Luxemburg which the anti-pirate legislation had not succeeded in suppressing. Radio 1's dominance over the other services was most pronounced between 9.00 a.m. and noon, while Radio 2's share was greater than that of the other services between noon and 2.00 p.m. Radio 3's share of listening was slightly greater in the evening than in the daytime, while Radio 4 claimed about a third of the listening which took place between 5.00 and 10.00 p.m.

The table below shows the quantity of listening, and its distribution among the various services, for different age and social groups. In terms of age, it is the teenagers who are the most omniverous listeners and their listening tends to be concentrated on Radio 1. Children under 14 listen little, boys less than girls. Amongst adults, listening to Radio Luxemburg is negligible; Radio 1 listening diminished with age whereas listening to Radio 4 increases. Radio 3 listening is confined to adults.

The pattern of listening amongst the occupied is much the

same for males as for females except that females listen to Radio 1 even more than males do. Since many of the unoccupied females are housewives whilst a high proportion of the unoccupied males are retired, their patterns of listening differ considerably; females listen three times as much and proportionately more of their listening is to Radio 1. Listening to Radio 1 increases sharply with each step 'down' the social scale while listening to Radio 3 and 4 decreases.

The last major development in broadcasting with which I was involved was Local Broadcasting. For years before the government allowed the BBC to launch experimental local radio stations the idea had its advocates within the Corporation. Chief among these was Frank Gillard whom I remember first as a young West-Country schoolmaster with a flair for broadcasting but who later became known to a much wider public as a War Correspondent. After the war he succeeded Sir Gerald Beadle as Controller of the West Region and later came to London as Director of Radio from which influential vantage point he was to oversee the establishment of the first eight local radio stations – at Brighton, Durham, Leeds, Leicester, Merseyside, Nottingham, Sheffield and Stoke-on-Trent.

The job of General Manager, Local Radio went to Donald Edwards. A Lancashire man of great charm who deceived no one with his masquerade as a very simple fellow who wanted everything explained to him in words of two syllables, Donald had come to Broadcasting House from the Overseas Service in Bush House some years before to grapple with the formidable task of restoring the morale of the News Division and convincing the rest of the Corporation that it, too, was part of the BBC. To the outsider the speed with which he accomplished these objects was little short of miraculous.

Donald wanted as much help as we could give him and, unlike some, was ready to put his money where his mouth was, providing the necessary funds out of his tight budget. Our local broadcasting exercise was inevitably costly because the work we did in each of the eight areas had to stand on its own feet. There had to be three viable surveys in each area; one just before the local station opened, to establish the 'before-using' situation; one after about a month of operation to establish

QUANTITY OF LISTENING TO BBC RADIO AND LUXEMBURG, (JAN.–MAR. 1971)

	Daily average per head between 5.30 a.m. and 1.00 a.m.					
	Radio 1	Radio 2	Radio 3	Radio 4	Luxemburg	Total
	hrs mins	hrs mins	hrs mins	hrs mins	hrs mins	hrs mins
Total population (excluding under 5s)	0 : 34	0 : 27	0 : 02	0 : 16	0 : 02	1 : 21
5–14-year-olds	0 : 19	0 : 07	—	0 : 02	0 : 01	0 : 29
15–19-year-olds	1 : 24	0 : 16	—	0 : 04	0 : 14	1 : 58
20–29-year-olds	1 : 11	0 : 27	0 : 02	0 : 10	0 : 05	1 : 55
30–49-year-olds	0 : 38	0 : 35	0 : 02	0 : 16	—	1 : 31
aged 50 and over	0 : 16	0 : 34	0 : 02	0 : 27	—	1 : 19
Boys aged 5–14	0 : 15	0 : 06	—	0 : 02	—	0 : 23
Girls aged 5–14	0 : 23	0 : 08	—	0 : 02	0 : 01	0 : 34
Gainfully occupied males over 15	0 : 36	0 : 24	0 : 02	0 : 13	0 : 03	1 : 18
Gainfully occupied females over 15	0 : 50	0 : 26	0 : 01	0 : 14	0 : 04	1 : 35
Not gainfully occupied males over 15	0 : 10	0 : 23	0 : 02	0 : 13	0 : 02	0 : 50
Not gainfully occupied females over 15	0 : 41	0 : 45	0 : 02	0 : 25	—	1 : 53
Upper middle class (15+)	0 : 15	0 : 27	0 : 08	0 : 32	—	1 : 22
Lower middle class (15+)	0 : 30	0 : 32	0 : 03	0 : 27	0 : 02	1 : 34
Working class (15+)	0 : 44	0 : 32	0 : 01	0 : 14	0 : 02	1 : 33

datum lines and one about a year later to measure progress. They were designed to assess local attitudes both about the prospective, and later the actual, stations and to measure the extent to which their programmes were being listened to and the source from whence their audiences were drawn. It was something of a nightmare to have to carry out twenty-four surveys in a matter of a couple of years with eight anxious Station Managers breathing down our necks and at the same time to maintain our normal services.

My retirement from the post of Head of Audience Research, already postponed for three years, occurred during this period but it was arranged that I should stay on in a back-room capacity to write up the eight reports. I was glad to do this though it wasn't easy to concentrate for at home my wife was in the last months of a terminal cancer. Shortly after her death I was able to fulfil a long-standing engagement – and as it turned out a merciful one – to teach for a term in the Communications Institute of the Hebrew University of Jerusalem, telling Israeli (and the many American) students about audience research, about the BBC and about public service broadcasting which it had been my privilege to serve for thirty-two years.

Index

Abrams, M. A. 16, 88, 136
Activities, The People's 105
Adams, Godfrey 198
Appreciation (Reaction) Index 116–18, 163
Atkinson, C. F. 14, 24
audience, definitions of 179–80, 182–3
audience composition
  age 125–6
  social class 124–5
audience measurement (*see also* Survey of Listening & Viewing)
  Early BBC experiments in 77–84
  discrepancies between BBC & TAM 177–84
  need for 73, 77
  of ITV programmes 174–89, 204–7
audience measurement, methods of
  aided recall 75, 89–94
  Dyna-Foto-Chron 73–4
  in U.S.A. 73–6
  meter 75–6
  simultaneous telephone call 74
audience reaction, need for continuous assessment of, (*see also* panels) 113–14
audience research
  early experiments in 58–72, 77–85
  early misgivings about 32
  Department 198–201
  plan for war-time 88–9
  post-war reorganization of 127–8
  publicity for 34–40
  role of 33–4, 40–2, 110–11, 135, 154, 174
  ten-year review of 136
audience size, factors determining 113, 121–6

BBC
  appointments procedure 19–20
  General Advisory Council 14, 39
  lunchtime lectures 38–9
  pre-war Sunday policy 15–16
  Public Relations Division 13, 25
Baily, Leslie 18
Barman, Thos. 15
Barnes, Sir George 135
barometer, general listening 84–6
barometer, variety 77–84
Baverstock, Donald 187
Beadle, Sir Gerald 37, 214
Belsow, W. A. 138–9, 171–2
Beveridge, Lord 134
Beveridge Committee 134, 201
Beville, Mal 86
Broadcasting and Everyday Life 127
Briggs, Asa 13
Brown, Farrer 168
brows, high- and low- 124–5
Burt, Sir Cyril 137

Cantril, Hadley 85
Cockburn, R. W. P. 22, 84, 104
Collins, Norman 198
commercial broadcasting
  attitudes towards 16, 110–11, 210, 212–13
  need of audience measurement for 73
  objectives of 19
comprehensibility of talks 139–42
Coronation, 1953 165
Correspondents, Forces 104
Correspondents, Hon. Local 88–9, 103, 105, 107, 110–11
Corwin, Norman 119
Curran, Sir Chas. 26

diaries, use of 145, 155

218 Who's Listening?

Drama Panel, 1937–8 58–61
Durant, Henry 94

Edwards, Donald 214
effects of listening/viewing 38, 70–1, 109, 148–9, 165–73
election forecasting 54–6
Emmett, B. P. 137, 151, 191

Farquharson, M. G. 21, 24, 26, 134
frivolity of war-time broadcasting 87–8, 97–8
Fry, Christopher 163

Gaetjens, Mrs N. 194
Gallup, George 16
Gardiner, Chas. 103
Gielgud, Val 14, 25, 58
Gill, Miss W. M. 126–7
Gillard, Frank 214
Gorham, Maurice 153, 198
Greene, Felix 85
Greene, Sir Hugh 85, 198
Grenfell, Miss Joyce 202
Grisewood, Harman 198
groups, use of 139–45

Haley, Sir Wm. 37, 111–13, 134, 136
Hamburg broadcast propaganda, study of 105–9
Handley, Tommy 99
Harding, Denis 138
Harrison, George 174
Hayes, L. W. 24
Hetherington, Sir H. 168
Hill, Bradford 38
Himmelweit, Hilde 168
Hoggart, Richard 125, 202
Hood, Stuart 187, 198
Hooper, C. E. 74–5

ITV
  audiences 177–89, 203–8
  need of audience measurement for 174–5
'images' of BBC & ITV 189–92, 204
interviewing
  for *ad hoc* studies 144
  for Survey of Listening & Viewing 90–7
  of children 151–2

Jacob, Sir Ian 175
JICTAR (Joint Industry C'tee for TV advertisement research) 176
Joyce, Wm. 104–5

Kendall, Maurice 172
Knight, Rex 138, 172
Knox, Collie 13

Lambert, R. S. 17
Laski, Miss Margharita 155
Lazarsfeld, Paul 85
Lee, Asher 42
letters, listeners' (viewers') *see* programme correspondence
Likert, Rensis 51
listener research *see* audience research
Listener Research Committee 24–5, 58, 84
listening
  distribution of 210, 213–15
  quantity of 208–10, 215
  role of 122–3, 157
Littman, F. H. 104–5, 137
living habits, study of 88, 105
local broadcasting 214–16
London Press Exchange 16–18, 88, 174

McGivern, Cecil 153–4
Macmurray, John 25
Matheson, Miss Hilda 25
Mayhew, Christopher 148
Miners enquiry 151
Mosley, Eric 104–5, 132
music broadcasting, studies of 85, 150

Neilson, Art 75–6, 86, 175–7
Newby, Howard 198
news broadcasting, studies of 150
Nicolls, Sir Basil 21, 26, 104, 114

Ogilvie, Sir Fredk. 88
Oppenheim, Bram 168

panels (*see also* audience reaction)
  early experiments in use of 58–62
  extension to television of 154, 158–64
  post-war organization of 128–30
  war-time organization of 114–19
Pear, T. H. 138
Pilkington Committee 201–2
pirate radio broadcasting 211–13
pre-broadcast studies 148
Press, Miss S. M. 23–4
Programme-Analyser, Stanton-Lazarsfeld 130–1
programme correspondence 22, 28–31
Projects and Developments 137–52
Psychologists, Advisory Committee of 137–8, 167, 171
Public and the Programmes, The 1958 188, 211

Radio Research Project, Princeton 85
Reaction Index (*see* Appreciation Index)
Reader Interest Survey 16–17
Reith, Lord 13–14, 61
Religious Broadcasting and the Public, 1955 150–1
Robey, George 14
Rodger, Alec 137
Ryan, A. P. 13–14, 17–19, 24

sampling
  emotional reaction against 43–6
  probability 47–9
  quota 47, 49–51
  selection of samples 47–51
  size of samples 52–3
satisfaction/dissatisfaction index 99, 210
Sayers, Miss Dorothy 118
Schramm, Wilbur 156, 170–1
Schwerin Corporation 131
Scupham, John 142
selective perception 167
Shaw, G. Bernard 14
Siepmann, Chas. 14, 24–5, 198
Simon, Lord 134–7
Simon, Lady 135
Somerville, Miss M. 142
Speight, Robert 118
Sprott, W. J. H. 137

Standing, Michael 193
Stanton, Frank 86
Survey of Listening and Viewing
  description of 89–102
  extension to TV of 154, 164
  inclusion of children in 151–2
  post-war reorganisation of 127–8
Swing, Raymond Gram 64, 86

Tallents, Sir Stephen 13–14, 17, 24
TAM (Television Audience Measurement) 175–86
tastes of listeners and viewers 65–72, 121–5, 160–1, 189
television and children
  Children and Television Programmes 169
  Nuffield Report 168–9
  Television and the Child 168
  Television in the Lives of our Children 170–1
Television, The Impact of 172
Television and the Family 173
Television public
  nature of the 155, 188
  size of the 153, 164, 186–7, 203, 207
Temple, Archbishop Wm. 14
Third Programme, Enquiry into market for 146–8
Thouless, R. H. 137
'Top Twenty', the 184–6
Trenamen, Joseph 132–3
Trevelyan, Miss Avice 24

'Uses and Gratifications' approach 149–50

Vernon, P. E. 137, 172
viewing
  and leisure 156–8
  distribution of 187–92, 203–8
  effects of 165–73
  quantity of 156, 162, 164–5, 187–9, 203–8
Vince, Miss Pamela 168
'volunteer bias' 79, 81–4, 144–5
vulgarity in programmes 98

Watt, John 78, 80
Whitley, Oliver 22
Wilson, Roger 18, 104, 110
Wootton, Lady 172

For Product Safety Concerns and Information please contact our EU representative GPSR@taylorandfrancis.com
Taylor & Francis Verlag GmbH, Kaufingerstraße 24, 80331 München, Germany

www.ingramcontent.com/pod-product-compliance
Lightning Source LLC
Chambersburg PA
CBHW070607300426
44113CB00010B/1434